"Sam Walton put _ _ _ _ business after serving our commu_ _y since my grandfather's days in the retail business . . . but I guess that's progress. If you can't beat him, I guess in a town this size, you have to join him . . ."

—Don Briggs, Former Men's Store Owner

"His most outstanding assets are his integrity and his feel for the people. He makes everyone feel good after he makes one of his talks. I don't know a rabbi or a priest who can do that."

—Charles Lazarus, Chairman, Toys Я Us, Wal-Mart Board Member

"If I'd known what I know now about how Sam Walton does business, I'd have voted against him when he proposed a new store in our city. Now I'm out of business and my wife is working for Sam down at the new Wal-Mart!"

—Craig Thorson, Former Mayor and Hardware Store owner

"He ain't like Donald Trump, always out to stroke his own ego. He's got too much class to be a Donald Trump."

—John Mayhall, Sam Walton's barber

THE SAM WALTON STORY

AN INSIDE LOOK AT THE MAN AND HIS EMPIRE

AUSTIN TEUTSCH

BERKLEY BOOKS, NEW YORK

THE SAM WALTON STORY

A Berkley Book / published by arrangement with
the author

PRINTING HISTORY
Privately published in 1991 by Golden Touch Press
Berkley revised edition / July 1992

ISBN: 0-425-13783-X

A BERKLEY BOOK ® TM 757,375
Berkley Books are published by The Berkley Publishing Group,
200 Madison Avenue, New York, New York 10016.
The name "BERKLEY" and the "B" logo
are trademarks belonging to Berkley Publishing Corporation.

PRINTED IN THE UNITED STATES OF AMERICA

10 9 8 7 6 5 4 3 2 1

The Author wishes to express special gratitude to the following publications for source material:

Financial World
Discount Stores News
Sam's Byline
The Arkansas Gazette
U.S. News & World Report
Benton County Daily Democrat
Columbian Missourian
Wal-Mart World
Business Week
Newsweek
Time

The Author would also like to thank the following who contributed pictures and graphs for this book:

Sam Walton
Hickman High School
Pleasanton Express
Wal-Mart Stores, Inc.
Private sources and the author's collection

To be rich is not the end, but only a change of worries.
                    —Epicurus, 342–270 B.C.

. . . And what lived on men?
Was it other men?
                    —Frank Cowperwood
                        of *The Financier*
                        by Theodore Dreiser

To Martha, my wife.
And to
the greatest businessman of all time,
George Austin Teutsch,
my dad.

Acknowledgments

No book can be written without the help of all the people behind the scenes. I'd like to thank my editor, Sandra Bybee, for picking out the rough spots. I'd like to thank John Rathbun for helping with our computer system. I can't forget Robert Chaney, Mary Isabella Williams, Agatha Jasik, and the late Alma Winters and the late Al Secrest for their teachings. For support over the years, Ms. Genevieve Moore, Ms. Margaret Dietz, and Mr. Frank Hause. Mr. Marshall Darby and Mr. Tommy Lange, men who employed me as a kid learning the ropes of the free enterprise. I can't leave out Mr. George "Mr. Mac" McAllister who helped me with growing up.

I'd like to add Ms. Sammie Franklin of the *Pleasanton Express* for the write-up, and the folks at the *Columbia Tribune* in Columbia, Missouri. The staff of the *Benton County Democrat* were helpful in Bentonville, Arkansas.

I'd like to mention Pat Lawrence, a fellow writer who supported me in this effort. This book would not have been possible without the help of my brother, Gary, who assisted me in the research and helped run our company while I tried to get the book published. I must thank the late Sam Walton for all his help, sending me information and pictures and letters of encouragement, even though he felt he could not be a part of the book itself. I'd like to thank Billie Crank for her support while I worked for Wal-Mart. She was a great person to work under while learning about the retail business.

I must add The Berkley Publishing Group and Ms. Susan Allison to the group of people who helped me get this book out. And my agent, Lloyd Jones, who kept pitching the book to anyone who would take a look at it.

Thanks Mom and Dad for all your support over the years. And thanks to all the readers who want to better themselves in business. Reading biographies of men and women who have made it in business is some of the best medicine during the struggle of making it on your own.

Contents

CONTENTS

Introduction

As a young boy attending college in Arkansas, I had no idea I'd be working for the richest man in the country when I took a menial job at Wal-Mart, store number 73, in the summer of 1978. Almost monthly, I'd see "Mr. Sam" Walton come into the store to check on his growing empire, but I never gave a thought to the massive machine he was creating. I was just another spoke in the huge wheel—or was I? Mr. Sam never let even a floor employee like me think of his position as anything other than vital. That was the kind of man I saw—exuberant, full of life, and ecstatic about his work. His "pep rallies" seemed corny. But his attitude toward his company was contagious. It was all designed to get a maximum sales effort out of his employees at the same time he was building a retail empire few will ever equal.

During spring break from the University of Arkansas, I began to look around for something to do. My grandmother lived in a small hamlet in Columbia County, Arkansas, where Magnolia was the county seat. Wal-Mart had a store in Magnolia and she suggested I try to use my spare time working instead of playing around like other college students. I applied and was hired. I didn't know who Sam Walton

was or just what was going on around me. I
didn't realize that during the day while I rang
up customers' purchases, stocked shelves, and
worked double shifts that I was helping to build
the biggest and most profitable retail chain
America would know in the 1990s. I thought
I was working for a man named Sam Walton
who happened to own a few hundred dry-good
stores in seven states. It seems that I was not
alone in this assessment. Retail leader Sears
and second-place K-Mart were also thinking
Mr. Sam was just another small but strong
retailer whose sales fluctuated yearly with
an ever-changing economy and world market.
They, like myself, were too close to the business
to see just who was coming up to the finish
line first.

After I left Wal-Mart, I regretted never
buying any of Mr. Sam's stock, which has
since split several times over. I remember Mr.
Sam asking me if I would think of making Wal-
Mart my permanent place of employment after
I graduated from the University. I told him I
had other plans and he said that was a shame.
I later learned that he was impressed with my
idea of labeling the front door of the store so
that the customer knew which door to enter
from the parking lot. This kind of thinking—
putting the customer first—was what Mr. Sam
was looking for. If only I knew now what I didn't
know then. Oh, well.

Many years later, as I watched the company I had once worked for grow tremendously, I began to think about what I could do to make myself a better businessman. What ideas and lessons had I learned from Mr. Walton's way of doing business? As I wrote them down, I thought I'd present them to my boss at the time, in the summer of 1984. Then the *Forbes* list hit the newsstands and I knew that the man I had met and worked for a few years back was more than just another retailer.

I began to think I could advance my fledgling writing career by putting down on paper what I perceived to be a formula I had learned while working those summers for Sam Walton. The more I wrote, the more I learned about this man's wonderful life, an inspiration to all who wanted to succeed in business, no matter what that business might be. One idea lead to another as I used all my research to build this biography of his life and retail empire.

Basic ideas of how to run a business and treat the customer became Sam Walton's philosophy of doing business. During the research for this book, it became clear to me why he hired energetic young college students to do the physical work at the same time he hired retired and elderly people to help the customers, giving the customers the feeling that they were dealing with someone they could trust. With a money-back guarantee on everything he sold, Sam Walton built a new way of doing business, a way that was lost by Sears and K-Mart and many others who tried to herd the customer through the turnstiles with little or no personal attention. When the employee felt comfortable with the boss, as we all did with Mr. Sam, we passed that pleasant feeling on to the customer. That built our return business up to a level no competitor could match.

But it took more than those inside moves to meet and eventually beat the competition. Sam Walton knew employees and atmosphere were just part of the fight. Retailing in the upstart sixties would demand more than that. Mr. Sam knew there had to be an untapped marketplace in a country of over 200 million. He found it in rural America. By keeping his 40,000-square-foot stores in small-town America, Mr. Sam built his empire around his competition. He knew the small-town customer wanted big-city products with buying-power prices. No one was giving that to rural America. Oh, there were stores, but they were not selling on a volume basis. They continued to try making their money off of their steady stream of traditional customers. They didn't realize until it was too late that modern customers wanted low prices every day, not just during a sale. Sam Walton knew it, and made Wal-Mart live it, with the motto "The Best for Less . . . Every Day."

By 1988, there was little known about Mr. Sam. By 1992, Mr. Sam would be receiving the Presidential Medal of Freedom for his accomplishments. His life teaches every American that the seemingly elusive American dream is still alive and well, all it takes is a belief in oneself and hard work. It seems that we all have been slacking off in that department during the "me" decade of the 1970s and the extravagance of the 1980s. I believe if more people knew of Sam Walton as a man who had a basic formula for success, that formula would rub off on everyone who read about his rise to the top. In an America desperately looking for real heros, I believe we could do no better than Sam Walton. There will always be the Donald Trumps and the Charles Keatings and the Michael Milkins, but they are all huff and fluff. Sam Walton, and men like him, are the very foundation of business in this nation.

Mr. Sam guarded his personal privacy carefully, but he never minded telling people the secrets of his business success. I should know: I used his basic formulas to build a million-dollar business of my own.

A footnote for those who wonder about true business greatness: On the floor of the New York Stock Exchange on Monday, October 19, 1987, men and women worked quickly, not knowing the full impact of what was about to happen. The week before, the stock market had lost 235 points. The Dow Jones Industry exchange continued its downward plunge, and as it did so, shock began to permeate the exchange floor. To confuse investors as well as members of the exchange, the market rallied in the morning and again in the afternoon. For those who discounted the serious nature of the downward spiral, for those who thought a sustaining rally would eventually come along to save the day, reality was a terrible blow. Nothing was coming to rescue the market. In the last hour the exchange was open, stock prices fell almost three points a minute, and in the last quarter of that hour, the drop was six points per minute. By the end of the day, the market had lost 508 points.

Pandemonium ensued.

In the worst crash since 1929, no company was left unscathed. Wal-Mart stock certainly sustained heavy damage that day. So did Sam Walton.

But another aspect emerged. It became a source of admiration, of discussion and of countless newspaper stories. Sam Walton had survived.

Never in the history of the stock market has one man lost so much in one day as Sam Walton. Being the richest man in the nation, and owning 39 percent of Wal-Mart stock, Walton lost $2.6 billion in net worth.

With a total personal fortune of around $8 billion, Walton's remarkable wealth was able to withstand the drop. Amazingly, Walton appeared to be calm, almost unflappable. Time and time again he had said, when quizzed about his vast wealth, "It's only paper."

This time Walton lost a lot of paper.

To put it in a different perspective, the advances on the stock exchange over the previous five years were astounding. Prices of stocks tripled between August 1982 and the week before the October 19 disaster. That five-year increase in stock earned owners two trillion dollars. But by the close of the day, October 19, one billion dollars of those gains would have vanished.

On October 19 alone, more than $500 billion was lost. And Sam Walton, one man, the richest in America, personally lost $2.6 billion of that amount.

He survived, and he endured with grace and style. The respect he garnered, the awe in which many had held him before, was greatly magnified.

Who was this man who had withstood the worst and was still a success? Where had he come from and how did he make his fortune?

Well, it started long before his birth in Oklahoma.

American Roots

1

Oklahoma Boy

The dry and dusty land of Oklahoma wasn't much to look at in the first few years of the twentieth century, when a young man named Thomas Walton came searching for a fortune of his own. Even though he acquired little in the way of money, he did uncover a land willing to yield a crop every once in a while, and he did find himself a wife. With her help, he discovered something greater: peace of mind for himself in a time America was changing to a more modern way of life.

Thomas Walton was a man of slight stature, and about twenty-two years old, when, in the early part of the 1900s, he decided to settle his new family down in the small Oklahoma town of Kingfisher, just north of Oklahoma City. Few others had settled in this dust bowl, but Thomas liked what he saw long enough to give it a try. Farming was a risky business, and a man with a strong back and a willing spirit just might have a chance to make a living at it. That was the hope of Thomas Walton, whose wife, Nancy, was expecting their first child in late 1917.

Thomas was the son of Samuel and Mary Layton Walton, a clan from the Ozark Mountains of Central Missouri. Most of the men in that family were hard-working, crusty, and set in their ways, with little time for much of anything but hard work and enough sleep to go out and do it again the next day. The clan was church-going and lived a simple life by choice, a tradition long established by the family. And there was no place for drinking or dancing or carrying on with the womenfolk. That was done in the privacy of the bedroom, as affection in the simplest form was not a Walton trait. Samuel and Mary conceived their son, Thomas, in the small Missouri farming community of Seymour.

It was years later, when Thomas was twenty-six years old, that he and Nancy began their family. Thomas was hoping for a son, just as his father had, to help out on the farm. In that era, not many men who lived past sixty years of age did so without boys to help out around the place with the hard, physical labor it took to run a thriving enterprise from the soil. Thomas had to do it for his father, and he was set in this way to pass the tradition of hard work along to the many children he hoped to have with his Nancy. That was the ethic of rural living in middle America in the early 1900s, built mainly on hard work and clean living.

March 29, 1918, was cold and windy, and Thomas Walton came in from the field, along with a few neighbors and a doctor from town, to help his wife with the birth of their first child, a son. Not much was spoken between those who waited for Nancy Walton to give birth in the bedroom. Words were few in those days, especially among the men. Most of the women knew the pain of giving birth and were mature enough to have a menstrual period, as it was also common and socially acceptable to be wed during a woman's teenage years. According to many elders, men and women rarely spoke of the workings of motherhood. It just was not a topic in many circles.

When labor was complete and the cry of a newborn rang out, those waiting outside the bedroom knew everything was alright. The men took a shot of whiskey, as did the doctor, and it was back to the field to finish out the day's work. But not before Thomas peeked into the bedroom to take a look at his new son, now resting in Nancy's arms with a full head of black hair. He thanked God for ten toes and ten fingers, and together he and Nancy decided to name the boy Samuel

Moore Walton after Thomas's father back in Missouri.

And that was when the richest American was born to carry on the Walton name and family tradition of hard work. Little did anyone know then that the boy would also take the American dream of making a living in a democratic society to the point of defining the very basis of free enterprise. How could they have known that, by the approach of the twenty-first century, he would create a new way for Americans to carry out their retail business transactions?

Although Sam Walton's keen business savvy came from several sources, it probably was not in large part from the dust bowls of Oklahoma. And even though they claim Sam as being a native son from the soil, Oklahoma was only his home for a few years after his birth. Even though Oklahoma was his birthplace, it did, in a small way through its simple way of life and constant hard work, pave the way for both Sam and Bud to forge out a life for themselves based on those principles.

Little Sam grew rapidly, and when he was five, Nancy became pregnant again. Seems like every time a man turned around in those days, somebody's wife was having a baby.

In 1923 Nancy Walton gave birth to a second son, a fat little boy the couple named James, but called Bud because his cheeks looked like two little rosebuds in spring. Thomas and Nancy were now well on their way to raising the many children they planned to have, much like the large families of their own childhoods. But then the doctor told them the bad news: There would be no more children. Nancy Walton was a small woman, and both births had been a difficult strain on her fragile body. The doctor sternly advised them not to have any more children, for Nancy's life might be at risk should she become pregnant again.

As it was in those days before birth control was commonly practiced, a doctor would perform a hysterectomy as a safeguard when having another child endangered the life of the mother. Thomas and Nancy were thankful for their two boys' good health and Nancy's life. They were to have no more children.

America in the 1920s was marked by changes that came so fast, a man could hardly catch his breath. There were cars replacing buggies, tractors instead of the horse and plow, telephones with direct lines, transatlantic airplane flights, and women voting. The country was moving on down the road of life, but rural America was slow to change. And Thomas Walton didn't like the changes he was seeing.

"Spoiled to the core," he said in an interview when once asked about his business in Oklahoma. "People began to get everything laid right at their feet, and the whole country was moving too damn fast."

Progress was the order of the day. Why, Nancy could even order the boys' shoes right out of a catalogue from the warehouse in Chicago. What would they think of next? One day it was airplanes, trains and automobiles. Who knows, maybe some day man would go to the moon. Nancy dared not say that aloud, or Thomas would think she'd gone mad. But if it weren't for dreamers like Henry Ford and Thomas Edison and even Sam Walton, the moon would still be scientifically unknown and inaccessible.

But life in Oklahoma was to end for the Waltons. Nomadic by nature, Thomas Walton tired of toiling in the Oklahoma soil, despite what the Farmer's Almanac said about the good weather to come for the year of 1923. Although he preached hard work as being the only solution to life's problems, he liked to use his head more than his back. Later on in life, after a final move back to his native Missouri, Thomas Walton preferred to shuffle paper more than he liked to shovel dirt.

He decided to move on and fulfill a lifelong dream of building his own business in the marketing world. Being a stern father who did most everything by the book, he assured the boys they would make new friends in Missouri, his native land. His longing to get back to a place he knew made the move exciting to the whole family.

Actually, they weren't much different from the TV Waltons of the 1970s. The Thomas Waltons were close-knit, and change seemed to draw them together in a stronger bond. When Thomas said it was time for a change, then it was time to pack the bags and move on. He was the definite head of the household.

Nancy also wanted the move, and for two reasons: better education and social interaction for the boys. She knew life on the farm would be good for them physically, but she wanted their minds to benefit from living in a community with other boys and girls their own age.

In 1923, the family of four moved to Missouri, not staying too long in any one town because of the economy. But Thomas Walton persisted in his attempts to establish a farm mortgage business in the towns where he and his family settled. As Franklin Roosevelt set a game plan in motion, so did Thomas Walton.

Conservative by nature, Thomas Walton was always extremely careful with his money. He saved automatically and knew he did not want to get caught without funds. And even though money was tight, it was not scarce in the Walton household. The Waltons had more than most and helped many of their neighbors out the best they could.

Finally settling in the small Missouri enclave of Shelbina, Thomas Walton began his travels to make deals, buy land and seed, help farmers bring in a crop and take his cut off the top of the sale. He also started selling insurance whenever he could get a dollar out of someone. Walton believed that, since everyone in the country had to eat, regardless of the condition of the economy, aiding the farmers was a priority in rebuilding the nation.

This was a concept stated by Franklin Roosevelt, and Walton was literally banking on the president's word that "This nation will not starve to death." And it was men like Thomas Walton who helped get middle America back on its feet. It just so happens he made a handsome profit in the process.

By 1929, when the bottom fell out of the nation's economy, Thomas had his family covered through his tight-fisted, penny-pinching way of doing business. He was able to provide food and shelter and a decent way of life while many were living on the streets during the height of the Depression.

Walton had saved a tidy sum of money, ready cash—another trait he'd pass on to his sons. This type of conservatism separated the Waltons from others who lost heavily. The rules were to keep a coffee can full of ready cash and have a plot of land with clear title when all else failed. Thomas Walton believed these two elements would keep him going through the tough times. And the tough times were certain to come if one waited long enough. While others were standing in line for soup, there was always a hot bowl on the Walton kitchen table. Thomas Walton made sure of it. Because of their financial security, life offered the Waltons more than a survival existence. They were able to enjoy a few advantages that made life more worthwhile.

When Walton was on the road one summer, Nancy decided to dress the boys up for a picture to surprise him when he got home. Sam was nine, and Bud was four, and she had ordered two neat outfits with shiny shoes from the Sears and Roebuck & Co. catalogue out of Chicago that would make the boys look their best. Ironically, it was Sam Walton who would later bring Sears to its knees and put the 102-year-old company on the verge of collapse in the retail world of 1989.

Nancy took the boys to the local pharmacy where the druggist was a part-time photographer. He put the boys against a blue backdrop and gave them a couple of gadgets from the store's shelves to occupy them while he set up the massive camera outfit. Shelbina was a small town, rural to the point of obscurity, and there was little in the way of recreation. Some said if a man didn't carry a Bible or a bottle of whiskey, well, there just wasn't much else to do. The local drugstore was the main hangout to hear all the gossip.

Even as the picture was taken, the Walton boys busied themselves with the gadgets. The photograph, taken on that bright, summer day, revealed a characteristic trait of Sam's that would bring him much future success. In the main picture, the one Nancy decided to take home to the boys' father, Sam is shown studying the gadget in his hand for its makeup and function while Bud is uninterested in the whole affair. It may have been their ages at the time, but their positions later on in life tell the story of two very different businessmen who both became billionaires by different means.

From the start, Sam was the leader, the genius. It is uncertain whether Bud would have attained his financial stature had he not been the brother of Sam Walton. Because even though the brothers entered the retail world at about the same time, it was Sam Walton, from those early days on, who made the Walton empire work. Sam applied many of the lessons he had learned in childhood from his father, and Bud followed him.

To understand Sam Walton's rise to the top of the retail world, Thomas Walton's business dealings in the early part of the Depression must be scrutinized closely. The elder Walton made hundreds of business deals at the beginning of each planting season. Farmers would put up part of their land as collateral for seed, and when the crop came in, Walton would get his cut from their bounty. But one bounty or one deal didn't make Walton rich. It was hundreds of deals and thousands of acres of crops which brought Walton his nest egg.

Should a crop fail to come, Walton acquired part of that farmer's land. As he grew older in Missouri, he became a crusty old codger to the many who knew him and dealt with him in business. This crustiness was a Walton trait, also passed down from one generation to the other.

It pained Thomas Walton to have to take a man's land from him when the crop failed to come in. But he was a fair man and usually let the farmer have another try at it. Through the years, these defaults added up to thousands of acres of land under the Walton name.

In the 1930s businessmen like Walton who were forced to foreclose on land were unfairly regarded as the real villains of the day. Even though they had "right" and "legal" on their side, they were frowned upon, much like many of the bankers who are forcing today's farmers out of their homes. Men like John Dillinger and Clyde Barrow became the distorted heros. They were men who robbed from the system, and the public perceived them as being in the right.

In reality, the bankers and money changers of the day, men like Thomas Walton, were the true businessmen who were willing to take a risk with the elements and a weakened economy to try to forge out a profit for themselves and their families. In Missouri in the 1930s and '40s, Walton was one of the most successful of these businessmen. At the time of his death in 1984, Thomas Walton was the owner of thousands of acres of farmland throughout the breadbasket of America, including twenty-three farms and ranches in the states of Missouri, Oklahoma, Kansas and Arkansas.

When Sam grew to manhood and began his retail empire, the lessons he had learned from his father were put in practice. He remembered his father never earned very much money off of one deal, but he made millions off of hundreds of transactions. This simple business philosophy is what created Sam Walton, the king of retailers. He never saw significant profits from selling one car battery or one set of dishware. But he did amass billions by selling millions of car batteries and dishware sets to masses of buyers. The power of numbers is what Thomas Walton taught his boys.

While Thomas was traveling the country making business deals, his family stayed in

Shelbina, Missouri. Life on the farm gave Sam Walton little to do. So he improvised on his own. During one of Thomas's stopovers at home, he taught his two boys to shoot the family shotgun for sport as well as for food. While Bud liked to fish more than hunt, Sam took to hunting with a passion, a sport in which he was still a proud participant at 72 years of age.

Much earlier in his life Sam Walton fell in love with the sport of hunting dove and quail. He spent many an afternoon and into the night out in the pasture hunting and bagging birds. Nancy would often have to come out into the cool night breeze to call him in for supper and homework. Basically a loner, Sam often entertained himself. With his father away most of his childhood years, and with Bud being younger and interested in other things, Sam didn't have many friends to play with out on the farm. Thomas Walton said in 1982 that he regretted not spending more time with his boys when they were growing up. But the love he showed them when he was home made up in part for his absence when he was away.

During one of many dove hunts in South Texas during the 1980s, Sam would tell reporters how it was his father who taught him to shoot and of the dangers inherent in a gun. Asked if he was a supporter of the NRA (National Rifle Association), Sam would only relate his belief in using a gun for sport and food. He did, however, offer some words of wisdom from his father regarding using a gun for protection.

"There is nothing more important than taking care of your wife and family and your home," the elder Walton told the boys.

"And in doing that, you have to use your best judgment . . . unfortunately you will probably have only a few seconds to decide, and the gun should be the last resort," Thomas Walton admonished. He taught Sam well. To this day, Sam Walton's stores carry guns for sale, and he was a silent advocate for gun safety, not control. Again, old-fashioned American values came into play. Common sense was also a Walton tradition.

Another interest of Sam's, while his father was out on the road closing deals and earning a profit, was to make money on his own. At the age of ten, the young Walton proved to be industrious and hard-working, sometimes to the point of obsession.

He milked cows and sold the milk to the local store owner. Then while he was in town, he delivered newspapers. After all, he was already awake, and there was plenty of time before school to get the route done. Sam thought he'd just kill two birds with one stone. After the fresh milk was in the cooler and the newspaper on the front lawn of many of Shelbina's residents, Sam was off to school for a day of book learning. When school was out, Sam would find other odd jobs to earn extra cash.

While his brother played stickball in the street, Sam Walton earned money in ways as varied as cleaning off porches, raking leaves or shelling peas. Whatever anyone wanted done, Sam was the boy to do it.

There is one thing Sam did in those youthful days for recreation. He became a Boy Scout. In the early days of the 1930s, being a Boy Scout was high on the list for young, rural youngsters to meet others their own age and gain friendships. Sam proved to his scoutmaster to be the all-American boy, full of energy and enthusiasm. Sam was also recognized for his talent as a leader.

Young Sam Walton consistently thought of ways not only to get the job done, but of how to do it in the least amount of time. Impressed by his work as well as his potential, the scoutmaster awarded Sam Walton the troop's highest honor. At the time, Sam was the youngest Boy Scout ever to achieve the rank of Eagle Scout in the Shelbina area. It is an award he remembered with fondness throughout his life.

The Eagle Scout award may also be the very one that set young Sam in motion to achieve more than the others around him, to be better than the best, to put in those extra hours it takes to be on top of the game of life. This achievement was a blueprint to Sam's life in the years he began to build his retail empire.

Leadership is something that comes from within a person, a person not afraid of taking on a task and finding a way to get the job done. From his early days, Sam Walton was exactly that person.

In 1988 a reporter from the *Washington Post* came to Bentonville, Arkansas, Walton's home since the mid-1950s, to interview the billionaire on his wealth and his beginnings in Oklahoma and Missouri for a cover story in the paper's business section. The reporter expected the richest man in America to live in the lap of luxury.

Instead, he found traveling to the small town of Bentonville, which is nestled in the northwest corner of Arkansas, to be difficult and tedious. He reportedly took a flight from Washington to Little Rock, then a small commuter to nearby Fayetteville and a rental car twenty miles into the Ozark Mountains, just to find the small town. He was shocked to see the home Sam Walton had built for himself and his wife. The large ranch-type structure, made of natural stone, was reminiscent of the home of a successful doctor, not that of a man with nine billion dollars.

The reporter saw a station wagon and a pickup truck in the driveway instead of a pair of Rolls Royces. There were no white-clad servants, only a small, aging, black woman who had been the Walton maid for some thirty years.

It was simply the resting place of a Southern gentleman, living very comfortably away from the hectic life he had built in middle America.

Actually, the reporter didn't get the story he came after. Mr. Sam, as he was known in town, was out hunting with friends in his old Ford pickup truck with the dent in the left side. Trying to salvage the trip, the reporter went into town to ask about this mysterious man. He walked into the local donut shop only to find Walton sitting with some of his truck drivers, still wearing his hunting vest and cap, drinking coffee and listening to their problems. Walton talked to him a little, but the reporter had already seen enough to write ten stories. Even though the reporter was expecting someone like J. R. Ewing or Blake Carrington of television's billionaire families who live week to week in the lap of pampered luxury, what he got was this diminutive man with a down-to-earth approach. No frills. No gimmicks. Just good old-fashioned American success in the truest sense of the word, staring him right in the eyes from underneath a hunting cap. The story nearly won the reporter a Pulitzer Prize.

An interesting and ironic footnote to Sam Walton's upbringing in the state of Oklahoma during the Depression in his formative years occurred in October 1987 when the stock market made its second historic thunderous plunge. Walton lost some $2.6 billion in one day. By nightfall, he'd lost a sum that would have wiped out many of today's richest Americans. Only then did people realize his massive personal wealth. But his conservative childhood in the days of the Depression in rural Oklahoma and on into the years in Missouri, together with the way he was raised by his father, proved that the origin of his wealth was, indeed, durable.

From an Oklahoma boy, Sam Walton would become a Missouri man in a land and a time ripe for raw business recruits. Roosevelt's ideas had turned the nation around, and the time was right for men like Sam Walton to grow into manhood with bright ideas in their heads. With the proper training from the right schools, and a little luck from being in the right place at the right time, Sam Walton would become the consummate future figure of retailing in America.

2

Missouri Man

The move to Missouri in the early part of the 1930s proved to be Thomas Walton's most enduring business deal, not only for his place in middle America's business circles, but also to mold and shape his son Sam into the great businessman he would become later in life. The move also pleased Nancy Walton. With most of his business deals keeping him on the road, their new home provided a more stable family life for the boys' formative years. Nancy was praying for it, and when the time came finally to give up the nomadic way of life, she was more than willing to do whatever it took to find a central locale to build a lasting home for the family. Missouri became the stability Nancy Walton felt the family needed. And it was a place which would be the Walton home for the remainder of Thomas and Nancy Walton's lives. Sam and Bud, however, would go on to new and different things, but Missouri would always be considered the true birthplace of Sam Walton.

The move was not without some nomadic ventures, business mostly on the part of Thomas Walton, trying to find his place in the sun. The family searched from town to town for just the right place to build a home and start a business, which by now kept the Waltons in money. They were a family without a home. The small towns they lived in for short periods of time were nothing more than temporary dwellings in the Walton lifestyle. After three years in five Missouri rural communities, Thomas Walton decided he could build and centralize his mortgage business in the growing college town of Columbia.

Shelbina may have been the small Missouri town where Sam Walton learned to appreciate business through the many jobs he had, but it was Columbia, Missouri, a thriving city ripe for new post-Depression business, that would prove to be the environment needed to mold Sam Walton into one of the greatest businessmen of all times. The breadbasket of America, with Columbia being the very essence of what free enterprise was all about, proved to be the fuel that catapulted the Walton boys into manhood.

When the traveling was done, Thomas Walton established his family in a large, clapboard house at 1309 Windsor Street, near his farm mortgage business, close to the heart of Columbia's new business district. People came to the city more and more to buy goods and services, and medical breakthroughs attracted thousands to the city-owned hospital for treatment.

As America began to learn and grow, so did rural America. Home remedies and homemade products used as substitutes for store-bought goods were being replaced at a rapid rate and the good, hard-earned money of rural America was fast finding its way into the city economy on a daily basis through the popularity of the automobile. America was on the move, and those who filled the needs of the people would not only be the ones to benefit, they would also become some of the richest. Thomas Walton was just such a man. Much later, employing the same principles of business his father used to become a millionaire, Sam Walton became a billionaire.

To know and understand how Sam Walton became the richest man in the United States, Thomas Walton's character is the key. He was a crusty, hard-edged man who had little time for anything but hard work, trying to make a dollar in a place and time where few were barely able to eat. His drive and his hard edge made him next to impossible to deal with. But this attitude is what made Thomas Walton survive in business. He was rough and tough. And he passed his inner character along to his two sons.

It was Nancy Walton, however, who gave the boys another outlook on life, far different from that of her husband. She provided the soft touch Sam and Bud Walton would use in direct competition with the hard edge the elder Walton had instilled into their minds.

Melvin Wells, a wrangler who worked for Thomas Walton up until the time Walton died in 1984, tells a tale of a man who, right up until the age of ninety-one, was a hard man to get a paycheck from.

"I worked cattle for old man Walton for fourteen years, and let me tell you, he was a mean son-of-a-bitch to work for. He didn't take any shit off anyone and he didn't care what people thought of him. He was almost always right and when he wasn't, he'd make it right," Wells offered.

"I didn't like him all that much, but I respected him. He never wrote me a bad paycheck and he kept my hours in a notepaper he carried with him day and night," he continued.

"One day, he dropped the notepad in a feedlot and I picked it up to carry it back to the house to him . . . but I sneaked a peek at what was so important in there . . . he had every business transaction like when he bought feed and how much so and so owed him all in that little book . . . hell, I thought he wasn't as organized as all that . . . but he was . . . I could never cheat that old man out of an hour's pay 'cause he'd have it all down in that damn book," Wells explained.

Columbia, Missouri, became a Walton stronghold, and he was one of the best known and respected businessmen in and around Boone County. His farm mortgage business was a solid lending institution, and his insurance office handled hundreds of policies each month, as the economy began to take shape going into the late 1930s. Much more important, Thomas Walton began to buy up land.

"You can have all the cars and dresses and stuff to make you look like you are rich to other folk," he would say to reporters during his retirement days, "but land and a good man's health are two of the most important things in life. They will never let you down if you take care of 'em." Thomas Walton enjoyed both right up until the day he died.

Thomas Walton took care of both. He wasn't a drinker, except for a nip now and then during the cold spells, or maybe a little wine with a meal. But he was never one to abuse his body. As far as land, Walton used his earnings to buy as much as he could handle. He never bought more than he could look after although it is well known around Columbia that Thomas Walton was well off. Nine out of ten owners sold to Thomas Walton, wanting to make a quick buck to buy a car or send a kid to college. And by buying forty acres here and one hundred acres there, Thomas Walton amassed a fortune in real estate at the time of his death. He was the Donald Trump of the 1930s and '40s.

Many remember Sam Walton's father as a quick-witted personality who made deals carefully, but swiftly. When the opportunity arose, he had the resources to jump on it. But all the pieces had to fit just right. When it came to saving money, Thomas Walton wrote the book on just how to do it. He kept a Luzianne coffee can in the floor of his office stuffed with cash, just in case there came another rainy day. And he didn't make any bones about his own personal wealth.

"It's none of anyone's damn business just what I got," he'd tell the press.

When the IRS came calling one day to audit his business, he told them the same thing.

"You got the tax return, didn't you?" he bellowed at the representative. "If you're calling me a liar, have a seat . . . if you're not, get the hell out of my office."

Just before his death, a reporter asked Thomas Walton about his two billionaire sons.

"Those boys have had every honor bestowed on them a man could want in this or any other life," he answered. "I just taught them how to work hard, and they took it from there ... guess they had the same kinda drive I had at their age."

"There ain't nothing fancy about us Walton men," he continued, "just plain hard work and saving your money. That's the real secret to the success of any man who's made a lot of money."

Sam reiterated his father's words at a class reunion held in Columbia in 1982. "He just taught Bud and me how to work hard and the rest would come in time ... that should be anyone's secret to any success ..."

1309 Windsor Street is now a student apartment house, having been sectioned off for rental property to off-campus students. Beside this structure sits a row of houses much the same, clapboard painted with bright colors, each with a small, neat front lawn. The old wrangler who worked for Thomas Walton lives in one of the houses, set up by his old boss before he died. Thomas Walton took care of his own.

"As long as you didn't try to cheat or steal from him," Wells said later on, "Thomas Walton could be one generous man ... it's too bad he didn't do more of it while he was alive, but then he'd probably have all the poor folk writing him letters or knocking on his door at all hours of the night and day, wanting money or something."

When a reporter from the *New York Times*, trying to get some background on Sam Walton, approached Wells about the elder Walton, Wells summed it up best.

"Old man Walton had his wits about him right up to the end of his life. And if you're asking if he left me anything in his will, well, he told me never to tell anyone about him, but I can tell you he could squeeze a Lincoln until the president cried. I'll bet he had the first ninety-five cents of the first dollar he ever made."

Even at the age of eighty-eight, Thomas Walton could be spotted in the parking lot of the local Wal-Mart outlet in Columbia, Missouri, gathering shopping carts for customers to use at the front of the store. One day, according to the store's manager who had taken it upon himself to watch out for the old gentleman, Thomas Walton stooped down to pick up a penny off the pavement and almost got hit by a car. The driver would have never guessed the man risking his life for that penny had a seven-figure bank account. Thomas Walton gave new meaning to the phrase "penny-pincher."

Funeral services were held in Columbia on August 17, 1984. Distinguished men and women of the city business community turned out to honor and pay their respects to the man who made his own fortune during his fifty-one years in business and around the city of Columbia. Sam and Bud Walton were present with their wives, as well as Thomas Walton's grandchildren and great-grandchildren. Thomas Walton was laid to rest in Memorial Park Cemetery. It was the end of a great business-man's life who made his mark in the bread-basket of America, living conservatively while pushing the free enterprise system to the limits afforded everyone who had the guts to take the bull by the horns and have a go at it.

Men like Thomas Gibson Walton, born and bred from hard work in the heartland of the most thriving country on the face of the earth, left a legacy of decency in business, even though there were some rough edges. But he left it all up to his two boys to take that same bull by the horns and have their turn. He knew they would either make it or break it. He also knew he'd raised them to be able to get back up no matter how the chips fell. Sam Walton took his father's advice and his father's way of doing business and taught America a thing or two about what hard work and drive can still do going into the twenty-first century.

A final tribute to Thomas Gibson Walton occurred in the summer of 1985, a few months after his death. The Columbia City Council had been trying to build a visitors' information center to promote tourism. The project had been on the drawing boards for some time and the money was now a question begging for an answer to get the actual building erected. Visitors were attracted to the city for several reasons. It was home to the University of Missouri and also boasted many fishing and hunting facilities. The council thought it should compete with other resorts lining the Missouri River just outside Jefferson City, which by the 1980s were beginning to look like a "Las Vegas of the Ozarks."

With permission from the voters to get the project off the ground in 1983, it was slow going trying to raise the necessary $500,000 price tag. After many months of exhausting work, the council could only raise about $300,000, maybe $350,000, but that was definitely the limit. It looked like the whole project would have to be scrapped. After Thomas Walton's death, the city leaders approached Sam Walton about a contribution for the center. Sam was willing to fill the gap of some $150,000 to see the center to completion, but he stipulated that it must be named after his late father. The city leaders, knowing the elder Walton had left his mark on the city over the past fifty years, agreed quickly.

But some residents didn't think it right for Walton to come back and literally buy a lasting monument when others, many who founded the city and worked hard for its development, also deserved recognition. Many thought it was rather tacky to have to buy in on the tribute to Thomas Walton.

Nevertheless, the Thomas Gibson Walton Visitors' Information Center opened in 1985, much to the delight of Sam Walton and those who knew Mr. Walton while he was in business in Columbia. Others just took it all in stride. Thomas Walton had made his mark on Columbia and his son was making a mark of his own on the city. In the end, both parties achieved their goals. Columbia got its visitors' center and Sam Walton bought his father a piece of history for all times.

Education was Nancy Walton's prime concern to the nomadic Walton lifestyle, and she pleaded with her husband to help stabilize the family long enough to get the two boys a good education. She wanted the boys to go to college, something very few middle-class citizens did in middle America in the 1930s and '40s. College was for the rich folk back East. When a boy or girl graduated from high school, usually by the age of sixteen, the boy took on his father's work and the girl married.

After the Walton family set up house on Windsor Street, school became Sam Walton's trade. And like everything else he attempted, he took the bull by the horns and rode it to the top. Just as he milked cows, delivered newspapers and became the youngest Eagle Scout in the early days of his life in Missouri, he utilized schoolwork and learning as his outlet a few years later. It brought him closer to his mother, as she embraced education to its fullest.

With grade school out of the way, Sam Walton enrolled as a freshman in 1932 at Columbia's Hickman High and became its fastest rising student. The red brick building, just down the road from his residence, would become a second home to Walton, and he spent as much time there as he did at his own house. He had to. In the years Sam Walton attended Hickman High, he *was* Hickman High. If ever a youngster epitomized the classic, all-American student, it was Sammy Walton.

Hickman was not unlike hundreds of other high schools in the 1930s throughout the United States. It was a two-story building with a basketball court auditorium combination on one end, a cafeteria on the other and a football field nearby. Sam Walton's legacy is still discussed by many students who write a theme paper about Hickman's most famous alumnus. Old yearbooks still grace the shelves of the school's library where pictures of Walton's past accomplishments still amaze students, both academically and athletically. Walton excelled in numerous ways. He was the head of many of the school's clubs and organizations.

As a freshman, Sam Walton was a small, scrappy kid with a positive outlook on life. He was well-liked and took on every task with a straightforward approach. He was a clean kid, never one to play pranks or drink or prowl. He was part of a family that wouldn't put up with such behavior. But he wasn't a boring snob either. He was every girl's brother and every boy's friend. Well into his first year at Hickman, Sam Walton took on the nickname "Sammy." It was an affectionate nickname for a young boy who had excelled rapidly in a short time, all the while befriending others.

A teacher once asked young Sammy Walton what he wanted to be when he grew up. It was a basic question often asked by caring teachers who saw something special in students like Walton.

"I don't really know," he replied. "Maybe I'd like to be the president of the United States one day, but I guess they don't elect many presidents from Missouri, do they?"

When Harry Truman became president years later, Walton, like many other Americans, began to realize America was actually growing up west of the Mississippi, and the possibility of his becoming president of the United States was closer to reality than it was to a dream. Only the teacher at the time believed what the boy was saying, for she knew his potential. She knew that this little scrappy kid would indeed do something someday, but like many others who knew Sam Walton in the early days of his life in Missouri, they couldn't put a finger on just what it was.

Later in life, Sam Walton rarely donated time or money to any political cause although he was considered the top of the "A" list by hundreds of candidates throughout the nation for congressional seats on up to the White House. His endorsement as well as any financial support from his massive Wal-Mart machine would virtually have put anyone in office.

While in high school, Sammy Walton wasn't much on getting to know the girls well or raising hell with the boys. In the 1930s, freshman were initiated into high schools all around the country by having to do crazy stunts such as eating cartons of raw eggs or rolling tractor tires down Main Street at midnight naked while girls passed by whistling. Some were made to climb to the top of the city hall flagpole with a bucket of paint, usually school colors, while the seniors called the local sheriff to help them down. Sam shied away from such pranks, participating as much as he had to. But he possessed, right from the start, more lofty goals which didn't include wasting time on getting a bad name around town. Sammy

Walton wasn't a bore, but basically, he was all business.

Sammy wanted his parents to be proud of him through his tireless efforts at schoolwork. His interests were all school oriented, except when he went hunting. And he was considered by many of the girls who went to school with him to be the best catch of all the boys. It was an innocent time, more innocent than the sock hops of the '50s. It was a time before the next world war and after the devastation of the Depression. It was a time of rebuilding and rethinking. Nancy Walton knew that part of rebuilding her family involved education for the boys. From his first years at Hickman, Sammy Walton knew it too.

Sammy dated often during his high school days, but no date was serious enough to lead to marriage. He had limited time for girls, unlike many of his male classmates. They made it a point to find dates while Sammy Walton dated when he could find the time.

At fourteen as a freshman, Sammy decided his goals were more important than taking a serious detour involving girls. He was mature far beyond his fourteen years. And all the talk his parents had done about doing well in school so his grades would get him into college made him work even harder. In those days, college was a complete luxury. A young man with a degree was the ultimate employee for any business, large or small. The Waltons knew this and wanted Sam to be that exception in Columbia, rather than just another farmhand's boy taking up where his father would eventually leave off.

Sammy Walton's list of accomplishments while at Hickman High reads like a fairytale . . . one about which any family of the day would love to boast. As soon as he entered Hickman, he began making a name for himself in athletics. At fifteen, he was named starting quarterback for the school's team, the Fighting Kewpies, a name derived from the wartime doll given as a prize at a local carnival. Sammy Walton, at 5′ 7″ and some 145 pounds, was tough and mean when headed for the goal line. His determination was only exceeded by his desire to be better than anyone else who tried out for the top spot year after year. He was captain of the basketball team that went to state when he was a senior, and in 1936, that same year, he led the Kewpies to the state football championship by winning every game. The purple and gold of Hickman was sure proud the Waltons chose Columbia, Missouri, to live in back in 1933.

Sports may have been Sammy's outlet physically, but mentally he excelled in the various clubs either as a member or as an officer. Some of the clubs no longer exist, a sign of the changing times. But while at Hickman, Sammy Walton participated in everything he could put into a fourteen-hour day. He was student council president, class president, member of the Forensic Club, Magic Club, Scroll Club, and Library Club, often holding an office in each. He was on the track team and was the star of the senior play entitled "Growing Pains."

Trying to do more than what is physically possible is what drove him at Hickman and continued to motivate him throughout his life. Putting in fourteen- to sixteen-hour days is an old Walton family trait. It would be the very basis of Walton's business foundation . . . long, hard hours as the main ingredient for success.

At his graduation in 1936, Sammy was the first to throw up his mortarboard and break into the Kewpie fight song:

Strawberry shortcake
Gooseberry pie
V-I-C-T-O-R-Y!

This bit of Walton spirit would become a familiar tradition as he rose to the top of the retail world with his in-store pep rallies designed to get the employees motivated for the day. He even danced and sang his high school song on the floor of the New York Stock Exchange in 1984, dressed in a hula skirt, when Wal-Mart stock reached an all-time high. It was something he'd promised his cronies he'd do if Wal-Mart stock showed an increase over the previous year.

I personally remember Walton using a pep rally just before we opened the store at the beginning of the Christmas season one year in Magnolia, Arkansas, store number 73. Although I thought the gray-haired old man had gone off his rocker and I thought it was queer as hell, the other employees who had watched "Mr. Sam" do his thing for many years were beside themselves with enthusiasm.

It was rather bizarre to see the richest man in the United States leading a pep rally personally to motivate hourly employees, but in the end, the store set a record for sales in one day. He would begin his rally by getting everyone to clap their hands along with him, then he'd break into a yell, like a Hickman High cheerleader:

Give me a W! (He'd wait for the employee response.)

Give me an A! (Again, he'd wait.)

Give me an L! Well, you get the message. I was somewhat embarrassed by the whole thing, but I was also in the minority. This man was selling himself and his store to his employees just as he had done all his life in every situation. When I saw all the old ladies of the lingerie department up on their toes in a frenzy, I learned a little about sheer motivation. Immature as I thought it was, it worked. And when the customers entered the store, dying to give Sam Walton their hard-earned money, I knew he was a genius at getting the only purpose of retailing accomplished: Selling merchandise. The bottom line was to sell merchandise . . . period. And no one in my lifetime has been able to sell it better than Sam Walton.

"He was clean from the word go," Bill Conboy said at a class reunion held in Columbia in 1983. "I've known Sammy Walton for over 52 years and he was a straight arrow. He didn't have to prove himself to anyone, he had better things to do . . . and while he was doing 'em, he proved himself over and over again."

His thoughts are echoed by another who knew Sam in high school. "That boy always caught my eye," Nelle Kitchens offered at the 1983 reunion. She taught Sammy Walton at Hickman and, at the age of 83, she was one of the only teachers left to tell any tale on Sammy. "He was the kind of boy you wanted your daughter to marry. He was a hard worker and quick as a whip," she recalled. "I taught him geometry, and he was at the top of the class. In this day when so many kids think education is for the birds and they drop out . . . they ought to take a look at Sammy Walton and see just what a good education and hard work can really accomplish in this world.

"But I wish Sammy had the time to talk to students around the countryside and tell them what a good education can do for you, but he doesn't. He's so busy these days with all those Wal-Mart stores I guess that is one job he'll never be able to do," Nelle Kitchens said.

Motivation and the formation of life goals were born at Hickman High while Sammy Walton learned how to deal with people. He mastered it at an early age and perfected it throughout his business life. Even in the 1990s, when he had a grand opening at one of the over 1,400-plus Wal-Mart stores throughout the breadbasket of America, Sam put on a show to motivate people into becoming customers.

His simple philosophy was that people like to hang around a kid who is doing something, as he did while at Hickman. In the same way, people like to shop at a store where something is happening.

Walton pulled out all the old tricks of a P. T. Barnum circus master when he opened a new outlet. He dropped live pigs out of helicopters, gave away huge amounts of balloons to the kids and offered free Cokes and hot dogs out in the newly paved parking lot. He hired a band to play patriotic songs while he led a march into the new store. And the cash registers played the most important song of all. With all the circus atmosphere, it's a wonder Walton wasn't known throughout the world. But remaining on a local level managed to keep Sam Walton out of the public eye.

While Wall Street thought Wal-Mart was just another small-town retail chain, Sam Walton was coming up their backside with record sales and astronomical profits. It took the movers and shakers of the retail world many years to wake up to his way of doing business. In time, especially during the 1980s, Wal-Mart began killing off the giants one by one. And it all started in Columbia, Missouri, at Hickman High where a young Sam Walton learned to be fruitful and multiply. With his strong family influence and the education he received from Hickman and the University of Missouri, he had all the tools he needed to topple any competition he would come to have later in life. His down-home ways practiced in the part of America he knew best gave Sam Walton the essential tools to slay the giants and bring them all to their knees going into the twenty-first century. Not only would he become a billionaire in the process, he would also eventually shake up the entire retail world.

The Hickman High School yearbook, class of 1936, tells the story of Sam Walton with a full-page picture of a young, jet-black-haired Walton as student body president with the caption below reading:

EXECUTIVE-Student President
Presiding over assemblies is just one of
the numerous duties of our President, Sam
Walton, affectionately known to us all as
"Sammy." In addition to routine duties
about school, President Walton serves as
our official host at school, and as our
representative when away from it. This
highest office in our school democratic
form of student government goes to the
man who earns it by his leadership, service, and ability. Sam Walton has gained
this distinction.

Life was centered on good times and hard
work until World War II became a threat. By
1936, Adolf Hitler was gathering his troops
to invent the master race. Middle America
was listening, but such an obscure little man
with a meek following didn't seem threatening.
Instead, it was a happy time, full of promise
through President Roosevelt's plans to bring
the nation back to the glory days of the 1920s
when Americans were interested in learning
to drive the new automobile or determining
the number of rings on their new party line
telephone.

Columbia, Missouri, like other average-sized
cities of the day sent many of its own to the
cause of war in the early 1940s. Thomas and
Nancy Walton knew their sons would have to

go eventually, but they also prayed the boys would complete their education first. During those times, a boy with good grades in college was the last person the armed forces sought for battle.

Many were volunteering in record numbers despite their parents' pleas. Sam Walton was, however, not one of them. The goals he had set for himself at fourteen were more important to him than anything else in his life, and he was determined to see them through. He wasn't afraid to go to war, but he believed in finishing what he started when he entered the University of Missouri in the fall of 1936.

Sam was set to study economics down the street from his boyhood home in Columbia. His mother persuaded him into entering the university so that he could come home on weekends. Freshmen were required to stay in dormitories in those days and the weekends nearby at the Walton home would give Sam time to visit with the family. Economics was a subject which fascinated Sam throughout his life, starting when he added up profits from his newspaper route and split proceeds from the sale of milk. Business was his life from early on, and having a father like Thomas Walton to lead the way, Sam couldn't help but be intrigued by the workings of the business world. Dealing with numbers also fascinated him.

Just as he had done at Hickman High,

Sam Walton excelled at the University of Missouri. He was a member of Zeta Phi fraternity and became president of his senior class while maintaining a 3.2 grade point average. Although he didn't participate much in sports, he kept his body in shape by playing intramural games with the frat boys. In those days, university life was filled with simple fun and hours of study. Since college was costly, parents who could afford to send their children didn't put up with any "goofing off." It was a serious business, this college education. Long talks from Thomas Walton made the boy realize the importance of getting this job done.

Sam was literally taking college by storm. He was an excellent student and the university provided Sam with a sense of learning about men and women outside the state of Missouri. While attending, he met people from all over the world. Professors and students from different parts of the country gave Sam a sense of just what it was to be different. This was a growing up time for Sam in that he was learning to deal with people, people with different goals and aspirations than his. It would prove to be a valuable tool for Sam Walton later in life as he began to employ thousands of these folks from all walks of life for his retail empire. The University of Missouri was as different from Hickman High as night and day to Sam, even though both were just down the street from his boyhood home.

It was from these two institutions Sam Walton received the education he needed, but neither gave Sam that sixth sense he would later possess. That would come from a combination of his father's business past and his own business future, learning by doing and using the middle American roots to know his customers better than they knew themselves.

Thomas Walton wanted Sam to help him out down at the office during breaks at college. Sam did it, but the war began to weigh heavily on his mind. The year was 1940, and Germany was moving about Europe freely, spreading war and bloodshed to the innocent people who were once neighbors. Sam felt the need, like many of his classmates, to put off the remainder of college and enter the armed forces to lend a hand. He knew he would eventually be drafted, and volunteering for duty would look better on a resumé for the future. In fact, unlike more recent conflicts, World War II soldiers wanted to go into battle. There were very few draft dodgers in the second world war. The recent war in the Gulf also brings to mind the type of troops World War II possessed in its ranks. Both showed their willingness to take on such foes as Hitler or Saddam Hussein of Iraq. After his graduation in 1940 from the University of Missouri with a degree in economics, Sam told his mother and father of his plans to go to war with the rest of America's youth. He was young and strong at twenty-two and ready to serve. But he was talked out of enlistment by his father. The elder Walton believed the war was about to end and wanted the boy to remain stateside if he could and take a civilian job with his firm to maintain a wait-and-see attitude. After December 7, 1941, Thomas Walton knew the real war was yet to come. Sam knew it too.

Thomas Walton had ideas that after graduation Sam would eventually come into the farm mortgage and insurance business with him. When the war proved to be more than a simple conflict, Thomas knew his oldest boy would have to go. And he and Nancy prayed the boy would be able to finish at the university before being called. They had heard form others about town that a boy with a college education could enter the armed forces with a higher ranking and maybe, God willing, take a stateside position in an effort to aid the men fighting overseas. It was their hope that the war would not escalate during the time Sam was in college. By 1941, however, their prayers were left seemingly unanswered with the bombing of Pearl Harbor in December. It looked as if Sam Walton would have to enter the armed forces, as he was the oldest of the two boys. The policy prevailed that the oldest male child, if he were in good condition, with a sound mind, would be the one to go should

America enter into a full-scale war.

The day the letter came, Thomas and Nancy Walton were somewhat prepared for it. The letter was identical to a thousand others sent by the government to families across America: "Your son is to report to ——— by order of the President of the United States." No parent is ever ready for a son to go off to war with all its uncertainty, but the Waltons had faith and believed in Sam's level-headedness. With the war an ugly reality, they also knew young men like their son would have to fight to defend the nation.

Sam took the orders in stride, and there was still a little time before he'd have to report for duty. With a degree from the university, it was possible for Sam to take a stateside position, since the Army had its eye out for qualified men to run the paperwork back home.

Between graduation and the time when he received the draft notice, Sam had about a year to kill. The retail world, selling and buying products, had always fascinated him from his early days of selling milk to the local merchant in Shelbina, Missouri. It was good, honest work, and everyone needed milk as well as other goods and services. He wanted to be that provider. And he got his chance in the summer of 1940 after graduation.

He drove his father's Ford automobile over to St. Louis to interview for a position with

the J. C. Penney Company, a growing chain
of clothing and appliance stores beginning to
expand rapidly all over the mid-section of the
country. He had visited one of their stores a
few years back and liked the way they did
business. A sales position had come about, and
Sam thought he'd be perfect for the job. He
waited in the outer office of the vice-president
for his chance to sell himself. With all the boys
at war, J. C. Penney needed men to aid them
at the in-store management level. Women were
hardly ever considered for manager, especially
in a men's store. Many retailers were out of
workers because of the war effort. Sales were
at an all-time low and the company had a hard
time trying to find good help. No sooner had
they hired a good man when a letter from Uncle
Sam would arrive and off he'd go. With a young
man like Sam, complete with a degree in hand,
the job was practically in the bag.

After the interview, Sam told the vice-
president he'd have to think on it. There was
a problem. The Columbia, Missouri, operation
had all the employees it could handle and the
store in St. Louis had no vacancies either. If
Sam wanted to work for J. C. Penney and
get his feet wet in the field of retailing, he'd
have to move to Des Moines, Iowa. Penney's
believed the young Walton boy had the kind
of talent they were looking for in a sales
trainee and quickly made him an offer of

eighty-five dollars a week to start. He was to report the following week to sell shirts and neckties with the possibility of advancement to floor manager, should he not be called on by Uncle Sam.

While Sam worked for J. C. Penney in Des Moines in the summer and fall of 1941, he often took trips to Columbia to be with the folks back home. It was now clear he would be called to war at any moment, and the time he had with his family was precious.

With a few days off, he decided to drive over to Clairemore, Oklahoma, to see a few relatives on his mother's side of the family. It had been many years since he'd seen them, and he felt it was time to get back to his roots just before he'd have to go away.

Sam made a few trips back and forth from Clairemore, Oklahoma, to Columbia, Missouri, in 1941 and early 1942 while awaiting his final orders to report for duty. It seems that while he was on a short vacation visiting relatives in Clairemore, he met a girl. Sam eventually quit his job in Des Moines and decided to spend all the time he could with this girl he'd met. And for the first time in his life, Sam Walton fell in love. Throughout his high school and college days, he dated often, but no one girl caught his eye the way this one did. Sam's parents thought he was grasping, worried that he'd be sent to fight in combat and eventually die.

Many young boys of the day believed in marrying and fathering a child before going off to war so they would have something to look forward to and a reason to come home. And if they didn't make it, they had a child to carry on the family name. Those uncertain times made many behave in ways they wouldn't normally act.

Sam Walton was no different. After all, there was no guarantee anyone would come out of World War II alive, with all the people being killed and reports of millions of innocent Jews being sent to death camps. It was a frightening time. The only thing certain was uncertainty itself.

Sam Walton was to report in the spring of 1942 to boot camp in California at a temporary base set up to shape raw recruits into fighting men fast. After six weeks, he'd proved himself to be one of the best at the training exercises as well as on the aptitude tests given to those with degrees who could be made instant leaders. Sam Walton never let them down and to reward him, they allowed him to take an extended three-day weekend pass before receiving his final orders.

Back in Oklahoma, Sam spent all his time with his new love. The object of his affection was a small, good-looking young lady who was a pillar of the Clairemore community named Helen Robson, the daughter of a wealthy land owner and banker. She may not have been the prettiest girl in town, but she had dignity and carried herself well, which made her desirable to more than a few men. L. S. Robson had made his money much the same way Sam Walton's father had done, selling and buying land and lending money during the Depression of a few years back. He was, just like Mr. Walton, a crafty, hard-driven man who looked after his children with a keen eye, especially his daughters. And Helen was the apple of his eye.

At the age of twenty-one, it seemed to Mr. and Mrs. Robson that the girl might never find a husband, as many of the other girls her age had already done. But not just any boy would do. He'd have to have that something extra. He couldn't be a simple plowman. After all, the Robson family was a well-known and highly respected clan throughout Oklahoma and northwest Arkansas, where Mr. Robson owned land and was a major stockholder in a small-town bank.

Sam and Helen fell in love almost from their first meeting. Both were quiet and shy, a contrast to their respective fathers. They came from well-off families and had goals in life they thought were more important than the world itself. When Helen Robson met Sam Walton, she decided to change her goal in life and be his wife and the mother of his children. It was a union which would last a lifetime, spanning the birth of four children and the establishment of billions of dollars of net worth. Behind every good man there is a good woman, it is said. Helen Robson and Sam Walton could be defined as role models for that saying.

Perhaps the best merger the retail world would come to know, their marriage was never front-page news in the sense of a business deal. But Helen Robson, who later became Helen Walton, was a very important part of the Wal-Mart machine during its building stages. There is little doubt Sam could have made it without her. But with her, he made it in a much bigger way.

The Waltons and the Robsons got along well right from the start. The similarities between the two families were astounding. Both possessed money and land and both had children with drive and ambition. The marriage between Sam Walton and Helen Robson grew in strength over the years, with neither money, greed or lust able to break it down.

L. S. Robson took to Sam Walton, perhaps like no other future father-in-law had ever done in Clairemore, Oklahoma. He had wanted his Helen to marry well and Sam Walton was all he had hoped for and more. And there was talk between Mr. Robson and Mr. Walton about their children's future. When the orders came in for Sam to report for duty, plans were made by all.

Just before Sam Walton received his orders from Uncle Sam, he came to see Helen one last time. And on Valentine's Day, 1943, Sam Walton married Helen Robson in the parlor of L. S. Robson's comfortable Clairemore, Oklahoma, home, complete with candles and cake and a huge family party. Sam wore his Army dress and Helen wore a lace wedding gown. After a quick honeymoon, Sam reported back to his battalion. He told his new bride that as soon as the orders came in, he'd send for her and they would set up a home of their own, no matter where the Army sent them, war or no war.

During the presidential campaign of 1988, Dan Quayle and Pat Robertson both came under fire for their subtle combat duty. It seems that their fathers, both wealthy and very influential, pulled out any and all stops to keep their sons from dying on a battlefield. Although there is no actual proof of either father using his clout to get a desk job for his son, the stigma was set in motion, and it hurt both men during the bitter campaign.

Thomas Walton was also a man of clout and wealth. And when the letter finally came in the fall of 1941 giving their oldest son thirty days to get his affairs in order and report to boot camp in California, Thomas Walton made a few phone calls to see what he could do. Just as in the case of Vice-President Quayle and television evangelist Robertson, little is actually known about those phone calls.

What is known, however, is that Sam Walton eventually received a stateside position. Many of Columbia's residents, both friends and foes of the Walton family, had their opinions, but there was nothing to back up their claims. By 1988, Sam Walton was just as powerful as Quayle or Robertson. There are very few native Columbia, Missourians who would actually speak up. As in the presidential campaign of 1988, no one source came forth with actual proof of any behind-the-scenes dealings by Pat Robertson's or Dan Quayle's fathers during the war years of the 1940s and 1950s (Korea). No one would go on record against Sam Walton either.

The talk L. S. Robson and Thomas Walton had about Sam's position in the armed forces can never be documented. The influence they had and the power to wield that influence can never be truly uncovered. But when Sam was given a special assignment as a communications officer behind a desk in Salt Lake City, Utah, in 1943, no one questioned how it all came about. There are no records to prove Mr. Robson or Mr. Walton aided Sam in getting this stateside job. While boys were dying, boys who were Sam Walton's school buddies, Sam was pushing a pencil behind a desk. Many say his schooling got him the soft position. Others say it was a combination of Robson's and Walton's money. Whatever the reason, Sam took the job as he had taken everything else in life and did the best he could at it. Given his unique character, there is little doubt Sam Walton would have taken to the battlefield just as his fellow schoolboys had done and would have fought his heart out. Money or not, Sam Walton took whatever was handed him and did the best he could with what he had. He didn't believe in complaining.

Sam's field of expertise for the Army Intelligence Corps was communications, but his down-home, earthy ways contrasted highly with the "rich boys" from back East who had also landed similar stateside jobs. He became a talker for the first time in his life. Taking care of problems for both his commanding officer and the recruits won him high praise from both ends of the spectrum. It would also give him the ability to communicate later in life while building his massive empire. It was hard to see who was benefitting more from the position, the Army or Sam Walton. After Sam attained the rank of captain, it was clear the Army was well suited for both parties.

Sam settled down in Salt Lake City. Helen joined him and they lived near the base in a small cottage. The honeymoon had been a success, as Helen was now pregnant with their first child. She gave birth to a son in 1944, a boy they named after her family's surname. Robson (Rob) Walton was to be the first of four Walton children over the next seven years.

At twenty-five, Sam was getting solid credentials from his work in the Army Intelligence Corps. These credentials would serve him well later in life with the many city and town councils he would have to deal with in order to open new stores in small-town America. When the war ended in 1945 with the signing of a surrender pact in front of General Douglas MacArthur by representatives from the Empire of Japan, Sam returned to the land he and Helen loved and would come to call home for the rest of their lives.

The Robsons wanted the couple to settle in Oklahoma, the birthplace of both Sam and Helen, but the Waltons wanted the kids to move to Columbia and enter into business with the elder Walton. Sam and Helen chose not to disappoint either, and they decided to seek a life of their own in a new and exciting land. They set their sights on Arkansas: the Land of Opportunity. Sam decided he wanted to be a merchant on his own, and with the resources from both sides of the family, he would have no problem giving Helen and Rob and the new baby on the way a good home. By moving to Arkansas, they would be close enough for visits to both families.

In 1945, after a short rest from military duty, Sam began looking around Arkansas for a location to set up a dry goods store. While looking in tiny towns about the state, Sam and Helen had a second son, John Walton. With money he'd saved from his service, Sam found a store in the small Arkansas community of Newport where the owner was tired and wanted a change. Sam packed up the old Ford and his new family and headed south from Columbia, Missouri, to a new life in Newport, Arkansas. The year was 1945, and it was also the beginning of Sam's lifelong love affair with the retail customer.

When he called upon his younger brother Bud to join him, he learned Bud had just taken a lease on a Ben Franklin outlet in Versailles, Missouri. It would be interesting to see how the brothers approached the retail business, because Sam's lease was also with the Ben Franklin company of Chicago, Illinois.

Although they started at the same time in retail, Sam would prove to be an abler businessman than his younger brother. In Newport, Arkansas, on a cold day in September, Sam Walton walked into his first store, ready to get his feet wet. With all he learned from his schooling in Missouri, and all the hands-on training J. C. Penney gave him, coupled with what he experienced in the Army, he held all the ammunition he needed to become a success in the retail world.

Sam may have been born in Oklahoma and raised to manhood in Missouri, but it was Arkansas, the true land of opportunity in the 1940s, where he would find his own place in the sun and a financial fortune no one had ever matched. He started from scratch in the breadbasket of a new nation shedding the shackles of war and embracing a new, fast-paced society, wanting to live life to the fullest. World War II taught Americans one valuable lesson in life: Live it to the fullest and get it while you can. For Sam Walton, if it became available, he was the first in line to get his share of the American Dream. What he did with his share would come to amaze the entire business world.

Building An Empire From Scratch

3

Arkansas: Land of Opportunity

It has been said that if the state of Arkansas were to be fenced off, cut off entirely from the rest of the world, it could survive completely on its own, given its resources of oil and gas, rice fields, cotton farms and chicken houses. Diamonds and other natural minerals would pacify even the most demanding, and the natural springs used for health purposes could make a man add years to his life. With rivers for fishing and plenty of hunting ground, Arkansas is a sportsman's paradise.

Why Sam Walton selected Arkansas to seek his fortune in life is no mystery. He chose it because of its low profile, high yield to change, and its abundance of retailing potential. Like fellow retailer William Dillard of the Little Rock, Arkansas-based Dillard's Department Stores, Inc., Sam knew the time was right to tap into rural America and allow the hard-working people of those regions the same products their urban counterparts had enjoyed for over fifty years.

He believed it was time to bring big-city products to small-town America, and Arkansas, with its state motto of "Land Of Opportunity," was the logical choice. While William Dillard decided to take the high road, building massive two-story retail outlets in the largest cities, begging to give direct competition to Sears and J. C. Penney, Sam Walton took the low road by saturating small Arkansas towns such as Newport.

In time, he would prove to all the retail world it's better to take a dime off of a million people every day than take a dollar off a thousand people once a week.

By bringing good products with a low price to men and women who would normally make by hand what they needed and save their money, Sam offered them a time saver. They saw that their time could be better spent making more money by bringing in more crops or raising more chickens. Men like Sam Walton afforded small-town America a chance to buy goods in much the same way as their big-city neighbors.

In 1945, Arkansas was one of the largest states in America in land size, but with very few citizens. The majority of citizens lived in small groups off dirt roads in rural communities. Arkansas, even today, has very few cities with populations over 30,000 residents. The residents of the state were farmers and logging people and a few worked the oil fields of southern Arkansas, near El Dorado where H. L. Hunt made a fortune of his own in the 1930s. Even today, there is only one large city, Little Rock. All others are no bigger than a good-sized Chicago suburb. With a state population of some 2.2 million people, Arkansas would hardly seem to be the starting point to a retail empire.

But Sam Walton understood that these people needed and wanted big-city products just like anybody else, and they had good money to pay for it. Being from just such a situation, Walton knew precisely how to change their retailing habits to buy from him. This is where his sixth sense was born.

Selling products, up until the early 1950s in small-town America, was left up to the local merchant. If a customer wanted something he didn't have, he'd order it from a catalogue, and it would be delivered to the store in a few weeks to be picked up.

Sears, J. C. Penney and even Montgomery Ward used their catalogue stores to get the rural dollar from the early days of the 1900s. But with the evolution of the telephone, the automobile and the television, America's buying habits were changing. The Saturday shopping day for rural America was fast becoming a daily occurrence. And they, just like their big-city counterparts, wanted the product "now." They didn't like waiting two weeks to get it. In Newport, Arkansas, in 1945, Sam Walton was prepared to give it to them and give it to them "now."

It was an exciting time for the young Walton family. Even though Newport, Arkansas, was not much of a place to start up a business in 1945—the population was small, and the people were basically poor—Sam was content with the deal he had made. It was a simple deal. The owner of a dry goods store, a franchised outlet under the Ben Franklin name with Ben Franklin supplied products, wanted to get back to his farming and ranching duties. His wife wasn't interested in running the store on her own and the couple's children were either career soldiers or married and had moved away to the big city. So they put the store up for lease and Sam got wind of it. With money he'd saved, Sam Walton took over the Ben Franklin store in March 1945 and quickly began to add products to the already solid line of goods the logging and farming community bought regularly. He didn't rock the boat and make drastic changes. Had he done so, he probably would have been run out of town. But he did change the way the store operated in more ways than one. Almost always, the customer came out ahead.

He signed a five-year lease, with the option to renew for ten. Both parties were happy, as the owner of the store had heard good things about Sam Walton. Although he'd never owned his own store before, Sam presented good references from his days at J. C. Penney and his service to his country. The owner liked that because he had a son who served in the war. Being an ex-soldier meant a lot in those days. It would definitely get a man's foot in the door, and Sam was able to use it to his advantage.

The year 1945 seemed right for free enterprise. The country was rebuilding businesses, and families were rebuilding their very lives from the ravages of World War II. The country was ripe for innovative ideas in retailing, and the trend of a faster-paced society made men like Walton sit up and take notice. The world was changing, and those who were able to see new trends in American life would be the multimillionaires of the future.

With the opening of Sam Walton's first Ben Franklin store in 1945 in Newport, Arkansas, the Walton family quickly became part of the community. They found a church to attend, and Helen learned that community service filled the many hours Sam was away from home at the store. She was pregnant with a third child. Sam was putting in fourteen- to sixteen-hour days, managing the store, ordering merchandise, and giving the people of Newport, Erwin,

Waldenburg, Harrisburg and Pleasant Plains the kind of hands-on retailing that would come to be a Walton tradition. Youngsters were getting their driver's licenses at 16, and families often sent the oldest into town for goods. Buying commodities when they were needed afforded a family an extra way of saving money, should the need arise. This was a trend that ultimately defined present-day buying by an American public wanting their purchases "now."

Helen Walton gave birth to another son, a plump little tyke they named after Sam's brother, James. While Sam was making a solid living with his store, brother James "Bud" Walton was doing quite nicely back in Versailles, Missouri, with his own store. Instincts in retailing that started to develop in childhood for Sam and Bud became sharper with their first stores. It is very clear that they helped write the book on retailing as we know it today. They just had the Midas touch when it came to getting the people what they wanted, when they wanted it.

The Ben Franklin Company in the 1940s and '50s was innovative and growing. They sold many products from different walks of life and even introduced overseas products as part of their regular line. In some aspects, the Ben Franklin company was ahead of its time. It offered fabrics, ladies' lingerie and toys, which were widely advertised, but hard for rural America to get without going into the city. Ben Franklin brought these goods to the people of small communities like Newport, and it was the leader in retailing dry goods in America.

But the downfall of Ben Franklin was its inability to see the changes which occurred in the early 1960s. There is little doubt this is one main reason Sam Walton parted ways with the company later on. They didn't think a discount concept would work. Even though they had buying power, they liked their profits. To change their approach would mean lower profits for the period it would take to shift the Ben Franklin way of doing business. Their inability to switch cost them the retail battle they would soon find themselves involved in with one of their own: Sam Walton.

In the five years Sam Walton spent in Newport, he made the store one of the best. People from all over north-central Arkansas came to buy products that were once only found in Little Rock to the south or Memphis, Tennessee, to the east. Bobby socks, white leather shoes, and hair tonic for that just-right ducktail of the 1950s made Sam's store the most desirable place to go. The previous owner also began keeping his eye on the store's progress and liked what Sam had done to it, especially in the areas of size, appearance and greatly increased profits. He would eventually deal Sam Walton his first lesson in business.

The previous owner had two aces up his sleeve. One, he was well liked in the community and was a hometown boy. His own son was coming home from the war, having been missing in action for years. The hero's welcome he received touched the hearts of the people of north-central Arkansas and brought back memories of a war not yet five years old.

The boy returned with nothing to do but work for his father. But the father used a clause in the business contract to oust Sam Walton from the ten-year option in order to give the Ben Franklin store to his son. When it came to one of their own, Sam Walton, regardless of how he was accepted in the past, was still an outsider. Through the local newspaper and talk about the community, the previous owner made it plain to Sam and everyone else that his son was entitled to take over the store when the lease ran out in 1950.

Sam decided to waive his renewing of the lease and move, but not before he learned a valuable lesson about people in business: Always sign a long-term lease and never let anyone or anything challenge that lease for any reason. And never let the public dictate your business, no matter how bad it may look. Much later on, Sam would use the lease example of 1945 as a basis for his hard-lined requirements at the more than 1,400 locations for his Wal-Mart empire. It became common knowledge that if one entered into a lease with Sam Walton, he'd better be on his toes. Part of the success of Walton's empire was a result of losing this initial lease, for no matter what the circumstances, 1950 proved the last year Sam Walton ever lost on a business lease.

Opening up another store in Newport crossed Sam's mind for a few days after the previous owner took over the store. But the market couldn't support two dry goods stores, and Sam decided to move on. He left Newport somewhat bitter, but none the worse for wear. During his five years of retailing, he built up a sizable bank account, enough to begin again.

One of Sam's more satisfying accomplishments occurred some fifteen years later when a new Wal-Mart outlet opened in Newport and put the war hero out of business for good. He purposely put on a massive grand opening at the site, and it was only a matter of time before the small Ben Franklin store gave in to his massive buying power. Every dog has his day and many people throughout the years have had their day while dealing with Sam Walton.

It seemed wrong to many of the people of Newport for the previous owner of the Ben Franklin outlet to use public sentiment to move Sam Walton out of the retail picture in 1950 in Newport, Arkansas. It definitely wasn't good business, as Sam worked long and hard to build the store up from its previous low. The opening of the Wal-Mart nailed the coffin on the war hero and proved that what goes around, comes around. It also showed that those who dealt with Sam Walton ought not to burn their bridges. He was a tough customer in his own right.

Back out on the road, with a wife and three small boys and another baby on the way, Sam and Helen returned to Columbia, Missouri, for a visit. L. S. Robson, who had his hand in a bank in Roger, Arkansas, offered Sam a job, and Thomas Walton again offered Sam a position in his ever-growing farm mortgage and insurance companies.

But the retail bug had bitten Sam in such a way it was in his blood. He had a genius for taking a store, changing it, putting in long hours with customer satisfaction a primary goal, and making money out of nothing.

Customer satisfaction. Sam liked the ring to that catch phrase and vowed to use it, not just as a drawing card, but as an actual part of his business. He knew that if he gave the customer his money back or fixed the problem with a product, that customer would return time and time again. He also knew that in order to operate a dry goods store in small town Arkansas, customer satisfaction was the primary point of business, since there just weren't that many customers around anyway.

While visiting the Robson family in Rogers,

Sam came across a man by the name of L. C. Harrison who owned a five and dime store he was willing to sell in a small Northeast Arkansas town called Bentonville, some fifteen miles down the road from Rogers. Mr. Harrison was old and tired, and for the right price, he'd sell.

Bentonville, Arkansas, in 1950 was larger than most communities, boasting a population of 4,000 residents. Even though it grew to nearly 20,000 people over the past thirty years, it still remains much the same as when Sam and Helen Walton moved there in 1950. It is somewhat remote, cut off from easy access, as it is tucked away in the hills that meet the Ozark Mountains. Sam and Helen found the residents hard-working, church-going people who rarely left town for any reason. Well, they never had reason to. Bentonville offered most everything they could want. It was just plain too far to Little Rock, and the drive to Fort Smith seventy miles to the south was downright dangerous through the bulk of the Ozark Mountains. Fayetteville, home of the University of Arkansas, was larger, but the merchants didn't offer anything new that wasn't available in Bentonville at the time.

Much of the small communities in and around northwest Arkansas were spotted with chicken houses and independent farms. A few acres of land had cattle on them. Logging was done, but the land was mostly in the high Ozarks and therefore part of the national forest. Bentonville was considered the largest city in northwest Arkansas. It had a town square with a Western Auto and a courthouse and two drugstores. Recreation was in nearby Fayetteville where a farmer and his family could watch big-time college football at the University of Arkansas. The Razorbacks were members of the Southwest Conference along with powerhouses of the day Rice University and Texas Christian University. It was basically a rural life, with the women sitting on the front porch shelling peas while the men worked on the family car out on the front lawn.

L. C. Harrison had owned Harrison's Five & Dime for about twenty-five years. He was a pillar of the community, and when he announced plans to sell his store to an up-and-coming young whippersnapper-merchant named Sam Walton from out of town, well, the people of Bentonville had many reservations. Outsiders were scrutinized carefully. They had to fit in with the scheme of things and the people who had lived in Bentonville all their lives. Walton also was skeptical at first, but soon began to make his way into the business community.

Mr. Harrison was high and firm on his price. Sam had to shell out $30,000 just to take over the business, its existing stock and its long-standing reputation. In order to expand, he needed $20,000 more for new fixtures, expansion and new lines of goods. He went to his father-in-law, Banker Robson, for aid in making the deal. He had big plans for the store, and he wanted to buy it outright. There would be no leases or deals on this one. It was all or nothing. Sam would either make it or break it. There was no middle ground.

Bentonville is a clean city, and the town square is the center of attraction on any given business day. The 9,000-square-foot store Sam decided on buying from Mr. Harrison sat in the middle of one side of the square. There was a vacant dress shop next door which Sam also purchased in his effort to gain more space. He wanted the store to be the main attraction. A town square designated the city as being the hub of government because most communities constructed that way were also the county or parish seat. Retailers realized early on that a location on the square meant business from surrounding communities.

Even today, merchants like Sam Walton try desperately to build near the town square for one of their locations. Going into the new century, these same retailers, in order to get more square footage per store, tend to move just outside the city limits on a main thoroughfare, also eliminating city taxes and ordinances in the process. It's a clever move on the part of someone wanting to be a part of the community while dodging the taxes and laws which actually support the community.

The courthouse sat directly across from Sam's new location. The Western Auto was within eye distance, as were the many shops selling dresses, shoes, and hardware along with the drugstore. It was set up much like a present-day mall, but without the roof. Every store was within walking distance, therefore keeping every merchant in line in his or her prices.

Sam was at a loss for a name. Since it wasn't a Ben Franklin location and it was no longer Harrison's Five & Dime, Sam logically called it Walton's Five & Dime. Most folk called the store the "Five and Dime" anyway, no matter who owned it. And Sam took to fixing up the store in a big way. He had the building painted inside and out and hired a St. Louis, Missouri, designer to give the place new fixtures and a personal facelift. This move impressed the wealthy members of the community who read about it in the local newspaper, The *Benton County Daily Democrat*. Sam stocked items never before available in Bentonville and personally worked sixteen to eighteen hours a day making sure the new enterprise had his personal touch of customer satisfaction at any cost.

The grand opening for Walton's Five & Dime was the biggest event to hit Bentonville in years. It would pave the way for the Walton way of doing business for many years to come. His philosophy of "people like to shop where there is something going on" held as true in 1950 as it did when he opened new Wal-Marts in the 1980s.

After the Waltons moved to Bentonville and built a home on a piece of land Sam bought just outside town, Helen gave birth to a little girl. Alice Walton became the center of the Walton household as the first daughter, but Sam spent little time with any of the children because of his obsession with the success of his store. His desire to triumph in the retail business was so great, there was little he wouldn't sacrifice. Many of today's billionaires will admit to being somewhat of a failure as a hands-on parent. Time is money, and it is hard to have both if they are equally precious to the successful businessman.

The gist of Walton's rise to the top of the retail business world was simple: He was a trinket salesman. There were only a handful of products in the Walton store of yesterday as well as the stores today which are necessities of life. His basic business tool was that if you sell low and in mass quantities, you'll sell out. Never give retail space to a product out of season, and know the buying habits of your area. For example, in today's Wal-Mart stores, bathing suits are sold much longer in Texas than in Wisconsin.

But probably the most important factor to Walton's business tactics was to put the competition completely out of business.

After a few years of a successful operation in Bentonville, Sam knew his formula was working and would be the same anywhere in the world. That formula of customer satisfaction and quick product turnover due to his choice of stock over his competition made Sam Walton one of the most widely known businessmen in northwest Arkansas in the early to mid-1950s.

In addition, the Waltons became a cornerstone of the community. They joined the First United Presbyterian Church where they stayed very active in the weekly church services throughout Sam's life. Sam was a deacon and Helen drove some of Bentonville's elderly citizens to services. She also joined various committees dealing with the church's direction. They joined in 1951 and quickly began a long financial relationship with the expansion of the church itself. Reverend Gordon Garlington offered in 1984, "I appreciate their [the Waltons] participation in everyday affairs because it strikes me strange that they continue to be down-to-earth despite their massive wealth."

Sam and Helen knew that becoming part of the community in every way would aid the store in its success. Being basically from religious backgrounds, it wasn't hard for them to do, nor was it a façade. Their honest upbringing is what dealt them their character, and all the money in the world can't change a person's basic background.

The Walton store flourished, but not without some controversy. In the early part of 1950, as had been the custom for many years, the merchants of Bentonville had a silent code of ethics. They didn't engage in price wars nor did they blatantly tread on any other merchant's product line. There were no rakes at the drugstore, nor were there bottles of aspirin at the local Western Auto. It was unwritten, but the times were changing. Keeping such a code would be hard to do in the face of competition and fluctuating economic times. After Sam had established himself, he started to change the long-standing tradition.

Sam's prices shot downward and he began selling items once reserved for other town square merchants. Other dry goods stores eventually folded under the pressure because Sam satisfied himself with a smaller profit and more business.

Stores such as Bill's Dollar Store, Gibson's Discount Store and even Ben Franklin would all fall in time as Sam opened up more Five & Dimes throughout the northern part of Arkansas and the southern part of Missouri. As his buying power increased, so did the heat on his competition. While it was the

American way of doing business, it was also the Walton way.

Soon, it was a common business trait of Walton's early days in retail: If he couldn't run them out of business, he'd buy them out. This strategy turned the Bentonville store into a flagship station for some fifteen of Walton's Five & Dimes throughout the area. The move was on and the fortune was building. By 1960, Sam Walton was a millionaire with no end in sight. Why other merchants didn't see what he was doing is a mystery to many. Why they too didn't gain buying power by expanding is also one of the biggest mysteries of the early retail world. Today, as in the massive quick oil change world, when someone gets a hot idea, the competition takes little time jumping on the bandwagon.

In the mid-1950s, Sam and his brother Bud went in business together, buying out the competition in and around Bentonville in a joint effort to become the biggest retailers in a two-state area. They started with the Ben Franklin outlets in nearby cities such as Harrison and Springdale, Arkansas. In a few years, Sam and Bud Walton owned fifteen Ben Franklin outlets with the promise to expand to as many small towns as possible.

Sam's desire to become a success in business was now a full-time job on its own. For many of the early years while building the company's base of operations, he rarely saw his wife and children and rarely went hunting, the other passion of his life. Only after the battle was won, did Sam know of the time he'd lost with his children.

"If there is one regret I have in my life, it's the time I didn't spend with my children while they were young," Sam said rather sadly at a 1984 stockholders' meeting when asked by a reporter if he ever had any regrets about his life. "And I can't say I was the best father in the world, but I tried my best." Today, the Waltons are close in spirit and business, but not necessarily in time spent in each other's company.

Having put many of the old shops out of business in the fifteen locations where he'd opened a Walton's Five & Dime, Sam was able to stock a wide variety of items because he was continuously building his buying power. He was fast becoming a valuable client in his own right to the manufacturers of everything from undergarments to blue jeans, a hot item Walton began stocking with the beginning of the "beatnik" phase among the younger set. He always kept his eye on the changing times as well as just who was buying what product. Baby sitting money for a pair of jeans was just as green as Framer Jones's with a million dollar spread. It was a safe bet that Walton was carrying whatever met both ends of the buying spectrum. And he sold only the luxuries of the day, things people wanted to buy but didn't need to buy. Common products included nylon hose at ninety-eight cents or a fourteen-carat gold-trimmed dinner service at four dollars and ninety-five cents.

Walton didn't believe in selling food items. There wasn't enough profit in food. He would rather sell the dinner sets and make a dollar profit per sale than bags of food with the same margin per sale. The Wal-Marts of the '90s carry some food, but not very much. Walton wanted maximum dollar profits out of his shelf space. Just as a good food store in today's marketplace sells magazines, batteries and toys combined with a deli and bakery to get all it can out of every paying customer while it "has 'em in the door," Sam Walton had that same philosophy. A monitor of a local Wal-Mart by a leading magazine revealed 98 percent of the customers who went into Wal-Mart walked out with a purchase of some kind—a tribute to Walton's knowledge of his customers' needs. Sell, sell, sell is a Walton policy.

Walton was a businessman who didn't like too many hands in his pie. He thought there should only be three principal shareholders to the final sale of a product in one of his fifteen stores: the manufacturer, the wholesaler and eventually Sam Walton. He didn't like keeping products on the shelf for long periods of time, gathering dust while the other two parties already had their money in advance. He liked the consignment idea but few wholesalers did business that way and even fewer manufacturers would ever consider it. When Walton's buying power became a point every supplier had to deal with it if they wanted to get their products in a Walton-owned outlet. And many had to "eat" their products when they didn't sell and refund his money to remain a loyal supplier. He had them over a barrel, pure and simple. Although he never had products on consignment, Walton always ordered products which could be returned for a reimbursement.

Walton also demanded rock-bottom prices from these suppliers. By keeping their price low, he could sell low and in vast quantities. The most important aspect to Walton's massive wealth was this simple business idea: Sell your products low, low, low. He would rather sell a thousand nail clippers at seventy-five cents than three hundred at one dollar and fifty cents. The public agreed.

When the customer finally caught on that Walton's Five & Dime had the same nail clippers seventy-five cents cheaper than the local drugstore, the drugstore had to close its doors or drop its price. It couldn't drop its price, and therefore it had no choice. There is power in numbers and Walton knew it had to come from the supplier. Make him sell his wares at his rock-bottom price and the rest would take care of itself. If the demand was great, raise the price for a higher profit. If the demand was poor, sell it like a poor man's product.

Sam knew his competition couldn't stay afloat because he was aware of what they paid for the same products he was buying. And he was becoming a somewhat cocky businessman with a thousand innovative ideas buzzing in his head. The pace was slowing down with very few Ben Franklin outlets up for sale. The slowdown in his plan to saturate the northern Arkansas and southern Missouri retail market was making him frustrated. He wanted results, and the pace was too slow. Walton was a bundle of energy, fueled by need and motivated by business greed. He wanted to rule the retail world and go head to head with the big boys, boys like Sears, J. C. Penney and Montgomery Ward. In time, they would all come to know this small merchant from the hills of Arkansas.

Some great consumer ideas originated in the late '50s and early '60s. Sam Walton's idea was simple: He wanted the Ben Franklin people of Chicago, Illinois, to back him on a discount retail store concept which would only sell products to the public with a small profit margin on each product. It would be borderline wholesale, but with friendly service and simple design.

The Ben Franklin people weren't interested. As a matter of fact, Sam had been working his Ben Franklin stores on this concept for some time, and they didn't like his profit statements. Believing he was hurting other Ben Franklin outlets by selling for less, they accused him of waging a price war with other franchise owners. He told them he could sell his products at whatever price he wanted. The contract never stipulated anything to the contrary, and Walton won the war of words. But he was growing increasingly dissatisfied with Ben Franklin and its ways of doing business. He thought about buying the entire chain out, but that would involve more money than L. S. Robson, Sam Walton and Thomas Walton could ever raise together. Such lofty dreams stemmed from frustration with the powers that be.

In time, Sam Walton would *be* the powers that be.

With fifteen stores in 1960, Sam and his brother Bud began piecing together what is now Wal-Mart Stores, Inc., today's largest retail chain. (Sears is second largest and K-Mart in third place.) It is a $44 billion per year retail giant with no end in sight. Even Sam's death could not stop the growth he started in the early days of the 1960s in small-town Arkansas.

While Sam and Bud were working on their

innovative retail formula, America was undergoing exciting changes. It was a time of hands-on business by the masters of consumer retailers. A young president, full of life, was now in the White House, and the United States space program began orbiting the earth as it amazed the world in a new, faster-paced society. The Korean conflict was behind, but Vietnam lay ahead. Music, freedom of speech in controversial books and records and interracial relationships were becoming part of everyday life, modern life. America was "growing up" to a faster-paced way of existence. In the retail world, Sam and his competitors saw nothing wrong with it, as a fast-paced society was a buying society.

An important aspect of life in those years was how to save time long enough to enjoy life to the fullest. Should a person spend all his time working or should a few hours actually be devoted to playing and living? People were becoming obsessed with time and began to value each minute of the day.

Today, people will pay for time. In the 1960s, people didn't have to because there were too many entrepreneurs willing to save them a few hours just to get their business. These business men and women are now the richest people in the world.

Hundreds of scenarios were played out during this important era in the nation's retail history. Ray Kroc was told no one would drive up to a window, speak to a plastic clown to place a food order and drive off to eat the food at home. McDonald's restaurants are now an institution throughout the world. The food chain even operates in Communist nations with options for even more expansion. At the same time, the Thompson brothers began to put one of their small convenience stores on every street corner they could find in every city they could do business. They also decided to keep them open early and stay late, say 7 a.m. to 11 p.m. The 7-Eleven stores became the leader in the convenience market for Americans on the move.

Junk bonds and a buyback in the late 1980s put the chain into bankruptcy, however. People were going so fast that buying that loaf of bread for lunch sandwiches and that gallon of milk for breakfast at the corner store was quicker than stopping at the supermarket on the way home from work. As it has happened many times over, with the exception of Sam Walton, 7-Eleven is in deep trouble, trying to stay afloat in the midst of killing off a wonderful concept in grocery retailing.

Sam Walton was using this philosophy of selling only the products the people wanted to buy on a regular basis. When women got a run in their pantyhose or men lost a fishing lure on the weekend, Walton's stores provided both under one roof quickly and cheaply. And he didn't keep banker's hours. Walton's Five & Dime was open every day, six days a week. Only the Sabbath was kept holy. In time, Walton sold products on Sunday, putting a frown on many a preacher's face.

While the small dress shops of the cities where he operated continued to offer selections that all looked the same, Walton brought in new, exciting apparel. He stocked car parts.

He was one of the first retailers to sell exciting music to the kids. If a buck could be made, he would make it. But he did draw the line on certain items, such as pornography. In time, that would more or less fall by the wayside. In 1985, he was admonished by a church group in Oklahoma for selling the compact disc, "Sugar Walls" by the Scottish pop star, Sheena Easton. They thought the music to be raunchy. Michael Jackson's records, with their suggestive lyrics, were also a target of many groups. Sam often walked the thin line in selling what the people wanted while trying to keep his stores in the family vein.

In the 1960s, girls wore bluejeans and sweatshirts instead of dresses, and boys wore western boots, vests and the ever popular t-shirt as their main wardrobe. Then along came the The Beatles. Sam sold whatever he could get his

hands on as fast as he could get it. He was fill-
ing rural America's needs and bringing them
the products their big city counterparts could
get on a daily basis. His stores truly were the
best places to pick up the new Beatles album
or latest fad, like the Frisbee, the Hula Hoop or
the Slinky. Sam Walton stocked the products
Americans were buying and, at the same time,
was leaving the competition in the dust.

He was one of the first Arkansas and Missouri retailers to learn kids liked college football team memorabilia. In Arkansas, you could
get University of Arkansas Razorback note-
pads, while in Missouri, you could get University of Missouri Fighting Tiger sweatshirts. It
sure made many a youth seem worldly while
still a student in high school. Walton's seasonal
aisles were some of the first of their kind to
appear in the early days of mass retailing. A
customer could buy a fan for summer, coats
for winter, masks for Halloween and tinsel
for their Christmas trees. But they would only
find it at the right time of the year. Space
was too precious to waste trying to sell fans
to Missourians in December.

Sam Walton continued his discount store
concept, even though he was a millionaire
many times over. Helen wanted him to take
it easier by 1962, as he was fast approach-
ing middle age. But he continued despite her
pleas. His motivation was as simple as the

mountain climber: "I did it because it was there."

In Bentonville, Sam was already a well-known retail giant. Helen couldn't put a finger on what drove her husband to do the things he felt he had to do, but she felt she had to do something on her own. She didn't know what to do during those lonely times he was away, tending to his bustling empire, but she had to find a way to slow him down. "I remember her telling me how worried she was about Sam's putting in fourteen to sixteen hours a day," recalls Bonnie Drake, a longtime Walton friend and fellow Presbyterian church member. "She was worried the kids didn't get enough time with him, he was away so much."

"I worked thirty years for the Waltons as their maid," added 93-year-old Elizabeth Dishmon, "and Mr. Sam was hardly ever at home. Why I didn't know whether to send out his suits or leave 'em in the closet, I never knew where he was."

"I never really got to know my father until he put me to work as a stockboy in one of the stores. Then I really got to know him," said Jim Walton in 1986, Sam's middle son.

Helen realized that just plain work was Sam's driving force. It wasn't women or drink or late night gambling. It was just plain old-fashioned hard work that kept him going. She soon gave in to his schedule and learned to live with his aggressiveness. Needless to say it paid off in the billions.

To get his discount store concept off the ground, Sam knew he'd have to live by his age-old ingredient, one that had served him long and hard: Keep the stores in rural America, towns and cities with populations of between 2,000 and 25,000 people, and never stray from it. He knew all the other suburban markets were saturated, and therefore, rural America was all his. He also knew he'd have to keep the stores at between 35,000 and 60,000 square feet in floor space. He pursued it with force beginning in 1962.

To get the discount store off the ground, Sam would have to find a starting point, one that was untested. Living up to his promise to Helen to keep the store close to home in Bentonville, Sam decided on nearby Rogers, Arkansas. He and Bud came up with a name, and in the summer of 1962, the first Wal-Mart Discount City opened its doors in middle America. With slogans like "We Sell for Less" and "Our People Make the Difference," Sam and Bud began merchandising items never before found in such large quantities in any small American city. Although Bud started Wal-Mart with Sam, it was Sam who was the driving force behind all the ideas and the store's eventual success.

By 1987, Bud Walton had limited involvement in the operations of the company, preferring to sail the open seas off the coast of his new home in Alaska. Bud has, however, let go of a few million here and there with donations to the University of Arkansas. Of course, as a Walton trait for spending $15 million, his name must be attached to any project. His Wal-Mart stock keeps him afloat and will for the rest of his life.

Striking gold for the second time in Arkansas came two years later when Sam opened a second Wal-Mart in Harrison, Arkansas, just down the road from the first store. By the end of the decade, Walton had opened eighteen Wal-Mart outlets in rural areas of Arkansas, Missouri, Kansas and Oklahoma. His saturating of middle, rural America was rolling right on schedule.

4

The Wal-Mart Way

Before the Wal-Mart empire began its phenomenal growth in 1968, Sam had to resolve a few past associations. The Ben Franklin company was growing increasingly aware of Wal-Mart's expansion. The fifteen stores Sam was operating through the Ben Franklin product line was becoming a burden to his expansion efforts. Sam offered to buy the stores from Ben Franklin so that he could convert them to Wal-Marts. The management hesitated because they would lose their hold on Sam Walton as well as the part of the country where they had done business the past thirty years. But they also realized he had the ability to return the product line and the Ben Franklin stores to them and then open a Wal-Mart across the street, thus becoming a direct competitor. They decided to sell. And they never entertained the thought of changing their outlets into a discount store concept. It was a decision which would put Ben Franklin virtually out of business some twenty years later. As Wal-Mart grew in middle America, Ben Franklin began to shrink.

The fifteen stores were converted over to the Wal-Mart concept and logo. Now called Wal-Mart Discount City, they operated under Sam's ever-increasing buying power. He began selling products never before offered through the Ben Franklin chain. Once out from under the roof of Ben Franklin, Wal-Mart expansion and profits began to soar.

Walton remained in small-town America with populations of 3,000 to 25,000 residents. He utilized between 30,000 to 45,000 square feet of floor space per outlet. By the end of the 1960s, Walton had incorporated Wal-Mart under the name of Wal-Mart Stores, Inc. It was after this event that Walton set out to become the largest small-town merchant in the nation. On October 31, 1969, Sam pursued his competition with every legal tool he could find. Putting the "other boys" out of business became almost as important as selling socks and shirts.

Sam decided to squelch such competitors as Gibson's, Bill's Dollar Stores, Winn's Department Stores, his old nemesis, the Ben Franklin chain and the ever powerful K-Mart, a chain so strong and innovative that even Walton decided to steer clear of their area if at all possible. By 1988, he had succeeded in dismantling all of them, by and large, except K-Mart.

K-Mart had been three times larger than Wal-Mart in earlier times, but by 1988, Walton expanded his chain to half K-Mart's size. He was also beating K-Mart at every turn with his personalized service and well-stocked shelves. He also decided it was time, by 1985, to go head-to-head with K-Mart, a move that had the second largest retailer scurrying for cover.

There is little doubt, with both Sears and K-Mart scrambling today to fight Walton's massive expansion into their sacred territories, that Wal-Mart will be the largest retailer in the United States for years to come. Wal-Mart surpassed the two business establishments mainly due to their inability to accept the changes occurring in the way the American consumer wants to be treated. The differences among the three retail outlets are extensive.

The Wal-Mart Way is a one-on-one battle. Whether it be price, personality, location or product, Walton knew just what the people wanted and when they wanted it. K-Mart understood Walton's way of doing business, but by the time they began a serious effort to take control of the situation, they had already lost their customer base to the new Wal-Mart down the street. K-Mart and Sears forgot the personal touch which had made them the leaders in the retail world. They believed they were invincible.

In 1974, Wal-Mart's CEO, Sam Walton, was gunning for them in every way he could. He searched for their weaknesses. At K-Mart, he found it in their employees, who by the mid-'70s were indifferent and placid towards the buying customer. Sears was much the same. Walton saw that a customer who walked into any Sears or K-Mart and needed help locating a certain product wouldn't get it. Target, a small chain which began to use some of Sam's personalized ideas by placing a telephone in each department for customer assistance, tried to get that one-on-one approach, but even that chain continues to fall short. Wal-Mart, by hiring college students and older people who wanted to supplement their Social Security checks by making a little extra on the side, found that this part of the work force gave Walton his personalized customer contact.

While Sam was buying old, run-down stores in small town America in the 1960s and early 1970s, K-Mart decided to place itself into a different retail category. The chairman of the board guided the chain to larger markets, staying away from the young upstart, Wal-Mart. Operating in cities of 25,000 or more, K-Mart found new life going head-to-head with Sears, Penney's and Montgomery Ward. But

the Wal-Mart way followed K-Mart relentless-
ly, no matter where it sought refuge.

K-Mart, with its aggressive automotive department and wonderful buying power in the
automotive field, liked the competition it gave
the local Western Auto and OTASCO, a mid-
West automotive supplier with retail outlets
in many states such as Arkansas, Oklahoma
and Louisiana. K-Mart believed Walton would
suffer greatly from the Sears, J. C. Penney
and Montgomery Ward catalogue outlets they
operated in small-town America, mostly in the
new strip centers designed to give the tenants
and the customer that "mall" effect.

What K-Mart failed to acknowledge was the
changing American buying trends. Consumers
wanted to buy now and take it home, and catalogue buying was fast becoming a thing of the
past. Only in the mid-'80s, with the introduction of the televised Home Shopping Network,
a call-in way of buying products that consumers use to avoid crowded malls, did the catalogue outlets get a fresh breath of air.

The twenty-year retail battle, starting in
1965, forced drastic changes in selling stra-
tegies. Personalized attention to shoppers was
a highlight of Wal-Mart stores. Another invis-
ible force on the horizon in those early days of
Walton's rise to the top was the introduction
of the local shopping mall. Sears and others
saw how important mall shopping would be,

and they signed long-term leases with various builders who promised high customer traffic. The gamble paid off. The mall in the '70s and '80s literally saved Sears, J. C. Penney and others from retail extinction.

The CEOs of the "majors" in retailing at first thought Sam Walton and his way of doing business in rural America was a flash-in-the-pan. Underneath the circus flair, the pig droppings and free hot dogs of Walton's grand openings and yearly promotions stood a concrete businessman. Walton was so conservative that the CEOs failed to see that the circus atmosphere was just a façade. Walton knew his potential as well as his limitations. It was simply that his competition didn't evaluate him correctly. By the time they realized this small retailer was entering their market right across the street, it was too late.

As Wal-Mart grew, Sam Walton began to withdraw his open, outgoing personality from the marketplace and become more private. He avoided "yes" men and he didn't like suppliers trying to buy their way into his stores. He granted few interviews, but he was accessible to favored publications, such as *Discount News* and *Forbes*, a magazine he would later come to hate. Reports of Sam's personal wealth began to enter into these interviews, and he wasn't one to discuss money, especially his own. Interviewers who asked Sam for a word were directed

to one of his associates, as he often referred to
his staff, no matter what position the employee
held in the company.

I held the position of associate, although
I was merely an hourly worker. The first
time I met Sam Walton, I was working in
store number 73 in Magnolia, Arkansas, in
the summer of 1978. He came up to me,
extended his middle-aged hand, and began
to ask me personal questions such as "Are
you doing well at the university?" and "Do you
think you'd like to work here at Wal-Mart as
an assistant manager after you graduate?" and
"What are your plans?" He also asked, somewhat rehearsed, "What is your overall grade
point average?" and "Do you like Mr. Lingo?"
(the location's manager). "Does he treat you
well and listen to any suggestions you might
have to improve your department?" Walton
was well-rehearsed and knew all the right
questions to ask any employee. Most questions
were two-fold in nature. By asking me about
the store's manager, he learned what kind of
job we were both doing. When he finished, I felt
I'd been grilled at a police station. Immediately,
I began to ponder his method and concluded
he was only looking out for his store's welfare
on a personal basis. He also wanted to get
information from the main source, the floor
employee.

When the publication *Financial World* named Sam Walton its CEO Of the Year in 1986, he was described as a "Southern gentleman" who allows his Wal-Mart "team" to guide the daily operations of the company.

In reality, Sam Walton never allowed his Wal-Mart machine out of sight for any length of time. Up at four or five every morning, he had coffee and donuts at the local coffee shop in downtown Bentonville. If any interviewer wanted to bend Walton's ear in the early days, all he had to do was enter the Daylight Doughnut Shop in the wee hours of the morning to find him sitting alone, usually, reading his newspaper.

Even though he was a multimillionaire, there were no Rolls Royces out in front of the shop, nor was there any sign of security personnel. It isn't Walton's style. He always kept a low profile.

At the coffee shop, Sam would listen to complaints from Wal-Mart customers as well as suggestions from his truck drivers, fresh off the loading docks at his massive Bentonville warehouse. This hands-on approach was Walton's way of doing business with everyone. Once a disgruntled customer who was nearly run over by an escaping Wal-Mart eighteen wheeler complained to Sam at the coffee shop.

"That goddamn truck almost killed me and my wife. You ought to do something about it,

Mr. Sam," he admonished.

And Mr. Sam did.

Today, Wal-Mart enjoys the best accident-free truck fleet in the retail marketplace, thanks to Walton's driving awards program. Even contract drivers such as Oklahoma-based J. B. Hunt & Co., Inc., must meet stringent requirements to haul for Walton.

As the largest employer in Bentonville, occasionally Walton would be approached by one of the town's less fortunate for ready cash. Given his background of hard work, he'd send the drifter on his way with a story about how only hard work can get a paycheck.

He'd also listen to residents who had ideas for his stores. Some would ask why the local Wal-Mart didn't sell meat to help keep the price down. They knew of Sam's massive buying power. Sam would give them a few reasons—very diplomatically—and they'd leave him alone. But for those who thought he wasn't listening, he was. He took it all in and actually used some ideas to make the company better.

Walton could be as nice as a preacher with a full house on Sunday, or he could be as tough, hard and cold as the situation warranted. By 1973, even though he had over 200 outlets, Sam kept his fingers on each and every one of them, either by phone, private plane or teletype. Once, on a surprise visit to a store, one of hundreds of such visits he made to keep his managers on their toes, Walton found a surplus of Christmas merchandise. Since it was using space in the stockroom in June, Walton went into a tirade that would make Leona Helmsley jealous.

"Old Sam knows how to raise the roof off this place," said a Wal-Mart employee of eleven years who worked in the distribution center in Palestine, Texas. "We have a love-hate relationship with Mr. Sam, he loves us and we hate him." The employee was in jest, at least to some degree.

He added that he'd seen Walton give the center's manager the "what for" for two hours over differences in procedures.

In a company letter to prospective associates who wanted to become part of the Wal-Mart team, Walton stated he sought people who were hard-working, dedicated, and innovative. He despised anyone who was lazy. He once caught an employee sleeping on boxed merchandise in the storeroom in 1972. After a glass of water to calm him down and an assurance from his store manager the worker would be fired immediately, he regained his composure. Making the rounds in the early days of the Wal-Mart empire was trying for all. Walton made it clear just what was expected of each and every employee, no matter what the position. He mellowed with age, but he still checked on the company daily.

As he built the company, he required everyone to work the same fourteen- to sixteen-hour days he was willing to put in. Those who didn't were not considered for upper management positions. He believed anyone not willing to put the company first, even over one's family, was not a team player.

Many of those team players are multimillionaires now in their own right.

Sam Walton had only one way of doing business: his way. To become a manager for any of the over 400 Wal-Marts at that time, the employee had to be a Sam Walton clone. His way wasn't necessarily bad, but there were strict guidelines to follow exactly in order to be considered for a higher position. And that's not bad either, considering that employment at Wal-Mart did have a certain amount of advancement opportunities.

As the Wal-Mart chain began to grow, Sam had to hire a reliable upper management team. After all, the chain was no longer just a meek little store in Rogers, Arkansas. By 1970, there were some 183 Wal-Marts spotted around four states. Sam couldn't physically take the time to see to each one, even though he had an airplane pilot's license and purchased a Piper to attend the grand openings of each store in person.

The men he hired were not well-known in the retail world. They weren't "blue chip" executives by any means, but they thought like Sam Walton and lived like Sam Walton, conservatively and quietly. Men like present-day President David Glass and CEO Donald Soderquist were not household names among the nation's retailers. Sam hired them for their backgrounds as well as their abilities. Flash and flair and a wild nightlife, making headlines, were not the kind of men Walton preferred. He wanted someone to get the job done, just the way he had done it. Sam was content to leave the flash and flair to the grand opening ceremonies of the one thousand stores he would come to open with the aid of men like Glass and Soderquist.

Sam Walton expected all his upper management team to adhere to one thing, even if they left the company. That was loyalty—to him, to the Wal-Mart company and to the cause of building that company up to the levels he knew it had the potential to achieve. He expected, received and rewarded the sixteen-hour days these men put in.

In the early days, the Walton way centered on being number one. Many accused Walton of plain greed, but his accusers were local merchants who had to close up shop, unable to compete with him.

A men's clothing store in Jonesboro, Arkansas, had succumbed to the new Wal-Mart on the edge of town in the early 1970s.

The store supplied the people of the city for over thirty years with their clothing needs. But customer loyalty died when the people found they could buy the same pair of jeans from Wal-Mart for three dollars less. Others say it was just sour grapes on the part of the old retailer. That retailer went to work for Sam Walton's Wal-Mart in the men's clothing department, the same store which put him out of business. This scenario would be played out a thousand times over the years.

There were thousands who Sam Walton had to fire because they didn't fit into the Walton way of doing business. If it meant missing a daughter's school play, then the employee missed the play. That was the Wal-Mart way. Nothing was more important than an associate's job at the local Wal-Mart, not even the employee's family. Although Sam Walton never said it outright, it was well known that Wal-Mart and its success was job one. Walton decided if he had to be away from his family getting the job done, his employees, those who wanted to advance in the company, would also have to put everything else aside.

Manager's jobs were precious commodities in the rural areas Walton operated. The local Wal-Mart manager was a pillar of the community and even envied. To not put in at least 10 hours a day meant any number of floor managers could take that job and prestigious community position away overnight.

During the Christmas season, when Christmas Day fell on Monday, a well-liked store manager sent a memo to Walton suggesting the store close the Sunday before. There was no reply. After an in-store evaluation of the manager's performance by an upper management team that regularly roams the countryside, the manager was demoted. The store's employees put a picture of Sam Walton in the employee lounge and threw darts at it until a new manager was placed at the store. They also began to call Sam "Scrooge," at the coldness of demoting their favorite manager just days before Christmas.

The Walton way of dealing with employees, hiring and firing, was quite remarkable. Sam's philosophy was simple: hire the right man for the job and get him as cheap as possible. Hiring college students, high school students through the local Distributive Education program where kids went to school half a day and worked half a day, and older citizens, kept employee payrolls lower than his competition. Part-time help was essential to the success of the Wal-Mart chain. And there is something to be said for the many employees who were full-time workers who bought into the company when Walton began trading stock on the New York Stock Exchange in the early '70s. They became millionaires even though they still worked the floor. These employees are still out on that floor or working part-time, buying time until the day they cash in their life's work.

Since Walton has no mandatory retirement age, he often hires the grandmothers of the rural communities to run his apparel and toy departments, and he will hire the grandfathers to man the automotive and sporting goods departments. Walton has always believed these people, rather than teenagers, get more respect from disgruntled customers. These older workers have a stake in the company, and they tend to show up for work on a regular basis, better than the kids he employs. Walton knew people liked buying from an older worker, and that they felt comfortable with someone who knew the product well and sold it with confidence. By using older employees who usually had a wealth of experience but were paid minimum wage, Walton was definitely at an advantage. An able-bodied older person can work at Wal-Mart until the day he or she dies.

The Texas "Blue Law," which has since been repealed, was always a thorn in Sam's side in his effort to enter the Texas retail market. In the 1960s and '70s, Texas regulated many products which could be sold and those which couldn't, on certain days. It was an outdated law made when a few merchants wanted to force others to close their shops on Sunday. For example, on Sunday a customer could buy film for his camera, but he couldn't buy a camera. The Wal-Mart stores did not operate on Sunday during those early years, but as competition increased and the Blue Law was set aside, Walton decided to open, after church services, from 1 p.m. to 6 p.m. All others followed suit.

Walton was instrumental in getting the laws changed in both Arkansas and Texas. His pressure, put on city councils where he promised to open a store and employ citizens, made many politicians stand up for retailer's rights to sell what they wanted, when they wanted.

Although Sam Walton was not a political man by nature, he used whatever it took to get his business off the ground. He rarely donated to any political cause or candidate. In 1988, as the wealthiest man in America, Walton contributed a paltry $10,000 to various groups, neither Democratic or Republican receiving any significant amount. Walton had other ways of getting what he wanted to better the Wal-Mart company. Giving anyone money for any reason was not Walton's way of conducting business in the public eye. He preferred to remain neutral when it came to state or national politics.

To make Wal-Mart a successful retail outlet in rural middle America, Walton knew he had to enter into areas where the old give-and-take method prevailed. He would give the communities the jobs, and they in turn would give him

Sam Walton

Boyhood home of Sam Walton, Columbia, Missouri

The Walton family, just after the move to Bentonville, Arkansas, 1951

Sam and Helen Walton at a Missouri grand opening, 1972

Sam and Rob Walton with New York Stock Exchange Broker in 1972

Sam conducting one of his famous "pep rallies," 1976

Sam Walton at Benton County Fairground, Stockholders' meeting, 1974

A Wal-Mart team

Sam talking up a game plan with employees, 1978

Sam had promised his employees he'd do a hula dance on Wall Street if the company had a pre-tax profit of 8.0% in 1983. It came in at 8.04% and Mr. Sam was true to his word.

The Walton family in Bentonville, Arkansas, 1983

A new, modern Wal-Mart as seen in 1989

concessions. Whether through tax abatements, utility hookups, or the waiving of ordinances, Sam demanded that cities give something in return for one of his locations. And they did. He had plenty of political savvy when it came to getting a store opened with the least amount of start-up cost.

Case in point: When Walton decided in 1984 to expand in the valley of south Texas, he needed to find a site for a large distribution center in order to get products to the new locations. By this time, Walton was already an expert in the workings of small-town governments, and he could sway city councils into giving him an incentive package, water lines, electric hookups, and the ever-popular tax break. In return, he'd hire as many locals as he could.

In the 1984 case, Sam pitted the Texas towns of Pleasanton, Gonzales and New Braunfels against each other in a bidding war of sorts. The winner would take home the grand employment prize. With the plunging oil prices and sour real estate market, Texas was hurting. Actually, the only true winner would be Sam Walton. The concessions the high bidder would make would barely equal the amount of taxes Sam paid, should the city council not decide the jobs were worth the waiving of twenty years of taxes. New Braunfels won the coveted prize. By 1989, with a small battle of the giants being played out in the town of some 25,000 as Wal-Mart and K-Mart both entered the marketplace, New Braunfels was forced to hire a full-time consultant in an effort to pacify the hurting downtown merchants. These merchants were getting something they had never had to deal with, competition from outsiders. Pleasanton and Gonzales may have been the lucky ones in this Walton deal in the long run.

As he had done so many times in the past, Walton came out ahead. By using a poor Texas economy, Walton took full advantage of it. Many called it a great business move while others, like local merchants and city councils, were now calling it shifty. But all the cities involved had an increasing unemployment problem, and they truly thought Sam Walton would be a quick resolution to the problem. Trying to pay their way in the deal, with old-time local merchants having to close up shop under the pressure of Sam's massive buying power, proved to be harder than first anticipated. Buying jobs is not always a good idea. There is little doubt Texas helped put Wal-Mart in business during the '70s and '80s and helped make Sam Walton wealthy.

The average taxpayer doesn't always realize what his tax dollars are buying when a private business such as Wal-Mart is offered tax concessions. But Walton made the deal look rosy in the many small towns where he opened a Wal-Mart outlet. If a community had to give up taxes for any length of time, the deal was a bad investment for the taxpayers. They are, in essence, putting free enterprise in business. And the chances of ever making it up, tax-wise, are between slim and none.

Without a doubt, the Walton way of doing business is to expand at any cost, and people are hurt financially as the Wal-Mart machine rolls across middle America. There is no end in sight. In order to see his dream of going head-to-head with K-Mart and Sears, Sam found the perfect connection in rural America, areas willing to let him run wild in the hopes of gaining ground economically.

And even though Sam Walton was not a politician, he sure had the politician's flair for words and manipulation of those around him. The Wal-Mart way was definitely one of self-promotion for self-preservation. Sam Walton was a survivor. By doing it his way, by the end of the 1990s the Wal-Mart discount concept will give competitors all they can handle and more.

5

Trouble in Black Arkansas

In 1962, at the time Sam Walton and men like him were putting together their fast-paced businesses, there was a tone being set throughout the retail world with some very fine lines. Not only was the entire country embroiled in a racial war, but also retail outlets were put in the middle of the war on two definite fronts.

Merchants were already used to the difference between black and white when it came to selling merchandise to the different races. The new problem, one that had been suppressed in the past because it just wasn't discussed in an open forum, was in keeping both races happy while remaining neutral through the whole racial turmoil. Walton and other merchants of the day were caught in the middle. On the one hand they wanted the black customer and on the other, they didn't want to lose the white dollar. Having black and white customers was becoming increasingly difficult.

While National Guardsmen were escorting black school children to class down in Little Rock, Sam Walton and others in retail were trying to remain neutral for the sake of their business survival. In time, they'd have to make a stand one way or the other and many businesses let it be known that they were not going to be a part of any conflict between whites and blacks. Walton and the rest of the retail community were caught between a rock and a hard place.

If they stood up for desegregation, many whites would move on to a store that made a stand for segregation. If they made a stand for segregation, they would lose the black buying dollar. Many merchants, black and white, were forced out of business altogether, and many had the opportunity to aid the cause, but chose not to.

Walton was one who chose not to. He was one of the many who walked the fine line of neutrality.

There were white cafes in those days, and there were white and black drinking fountains as well as white and black laundromats. And there were the white and black stores. It was unheard of for a white woman to shop in a colored store and vice versa. Even if the store didn't have the usual sign out front announcing "Whites Only," everyone in towns across the state knew their "place." Walton and other merchants had difficulty trying to get a green buck out of black and white people who didn't want to be seen in town with one another.

In many small towns like Newport and Bentonville during those early years, there were generally two food stores. But there was only one automotive store, one drug store and one dry goods store. Walton fell into the last category and trying to sell products to both races was a job in itself.

The automotive and hardware store didn't have much of a problem. Many black and white men didn't divide along racial lines when working side by side in the hot Arkansas sun. Also, many stores were selling to blacks out of the back door. The local pharmacist sold his prescriptions directly to the black doctor to avoid any confrontations in his store. The local hardware man told the blacks that he'd open an hour early and stay open an hour later so they could shop in peace. After the civil rights movement of the mid-60s, merchants were in for the fight of their lives just to keep peace in their communities and to make a profit. A merchant quickly found he couldn't have his cake and eat it too. It was either sell to the white population or become a store strictly for blacks.

By the time the civil rights movement began to sweep the south, the Wal-Mart retail chain also began a sweep of its own. In light of the tensions surrounding him, Walton found it very difficult to hire blacks. White customers didn't want to shop at a store where blacks were even employed. The hatred was deep and real, and Walton was caught up in what was right and what was monetarily beneficial. He went for the money, as did many of his competitors. They had to make a living and didn't want to be part of what they called a political tug of war between the races.

Walton began to shift his black employees to different duties, duties which would keep them out of view of the predominantly white buying public. And he was relieved for the first time in his life at the new competition which began to sprout up by black merchants taking some of the heat off his stores. Sam changed his policy as the war on racism changed, but during the most heated times of the turmoil, he didn't employ blacks out on the floor of his stores to sell merchandise to white customers. (*Much later, in 1973, while my black roommate worked at the local Wal-Mart, he experienced racism while working for Sam Walton.*) Even though a town might be seventy per cent black, Walton hired more whites to work the store front and kept the blacks back in the warehouse or assigned to janitorial duties at night. (*At the Wal-Mart I worked in in Magnolia, Arkansas, in 1978, only six blacks worked the floor while the city's population was at least fifty to sixty per cent black*.) And even after the 1964 Civil Rights Act, which described to all men and women a person could not be discriminated against because of sex, race or religious beliefs, Sam Walton and others found a way to keep whites pacified while at the same time employing qualified blacks in their workforce. It wasn't easy, but Walton found a way to pull it off. K-Mart and Sears were also having their problems, too. It wasn't just a Wal-Mart situation.

A basic scenario to the solving of the racial issue Walton used seemed satisfactory and stopped many a discrimination suit. Walton would hire a black man or woman and put that person on the floor as a sales trainee with duties to stock the shelves. They were instructed to wait on a black customer and leave the white customer to the white clerk. If there wasn't a white clerk present, they should wait until the white customer asked for assistance. Walton allowed the white customer to select his clerk, knowing full well many of the citizens wouldn't ask for, much less buy a garment from a black clerk. By playing the word game, he found out who his customers were from the inside out. It helped keep him in line with the new law, and his sales were increasing as racial tensions from local citizens began to decrease. The success of the law lies in the fact that more whites and blacks were law-abiding than not. In the retail world, the success of the law turned into profits for the merchants forced finally to deal with an age-old problem of black and white stores.

In the mid-1960s at a time when Walton's outlets were growing at an alarming rate in eleven rural states, some 195 stores in a 500-mile radius, Walton proved to many he was no champion of the minority groups (blacks in Arkansas and Louisiana, Mexican-Americans in Texas). After entering the Texas marketplace, he hired illegal aliens from Mexico for the loading docks in Palestine, and later in the valley of south Texas. These workers provided Walton with cheap labor and larger profits. Walton was not alone, as hiring aliens in Texas came with the territory of doing business so near such a desperate country as Mexico. And until white men and women became unemployed on a massive scale due to a downturn in the oil business, "wetbacks" as they were called, made up a large proportion of the work force for many companies such as Wal-Mart. After the complaints began because there weren't enough jobs to go around for both Mexicans and American citizens, the laws were beginning to be enforced more directly in the form of fines. By the 1970s, a man such as Sam Walton could be fined as much as a thousand dollars per illegal alien, should they be caught working without a permit.

After President Ronald Reagan's amnesty program was instigated in the 1980s, and with the threat of a $1,000 fine per violation, Walton chose to hire only Mexican nationals who held a visa or were in the process of obtaining United States citizenship.

Sam Walton experienced little racism in today's marketplace. Wal-Mart Stores, Inc., remains a haven for the white work force. Sam continued to favor the white work force over hiring blacks, even though many of the cities he operated in were predominantly black. Although it was not a conscious effort on the part of Sam Walton or his staff as it relates to hiring, a random survey proved Wal-Mart did indeed hire more whites than any other race, regardless of the town's population figures as they related to black and white.

There was only one instance in the forty years of retail business Sam Walton enjoyed where he actually made an effort to aid anyone in the black community. In Columbia, Missouri, in 1980, Sam gave twenty black kids twenty dollars each to buy toys for Christmas at one of his Wal-Mart outlets. A nice gesture on the surface, and it was a wealth of positive publicity for Walton. Having been confronted in the past by many local NAACP chapters for donations and aid, he felt it would pacify them long enough to show America he was a wealthy man who cared. Never before in the history of business has such a wealthy man reaped such rewards of positive publicity from such a small gesture. If he'd paid for the kids to go to college, he very well could have reached sainthood. A couple thousand dollars to a man who has billions does not qualify a man for sainthood. But twenty dollars for toys for poor, black kids revealed a lack of understanding on Sam Walton's part.

He also got his twenty dollars back and was out only the cost of the toys themselves. With his massive buying power in 1980, the total sum of his contribution to the poor of Columbia was $100. It is truly amazing what $100 bought Walton in the form of positive publicity. When the richest man in America gives a kid $20 to buy toys in his store, that's big news. When it's Sam Walton doing the deed, the real winner turns out to be Sam Walton.

6

From Dream to Massive Reality

By 1970, Wal-Mart was growing into a large company with its first distribution center opening in Bentonville. Within the complex, Walton headquartered his chain of stores and built a row of offices for himself and the upper management team he had assembled. That team consisted of about thirty upper management personnel, legal staff, public relations department and secretaries, in addition to one hundred or so men and women hired to count the daily take from some four hundred stores.

The entire operation was incorporated October 31, 1969, under the legal name of Wal-Mart Stores Incorporated. He had over a hundred stores in eleven states and was growing at the rate of twenty stores a year. Walton began offering stock options, and Wal-Mart stock traded over the counter in October 1970. The changes in the company prompted others to take a second look at this small-town merchant.

By mid-1970, Wal-Mart became a publicly held company with stocks trading over the counter until August 1972, when it was approved and listed on the New York Stock Exchange. The Ben Franklin stores, long a sore spot to Walton in that they were regulated by outsiders, were phased out and became Wal-Marts in 1976. By the end of 1979, Wal-Mart had grown to a massive 276 outlets. But they remained in small-town America and at an average of 45,000 square feet per store.

Sam Walton's dream was becoming a nightmare to many of his competitors. They saw him coming and had no way of stopping his massive growth. Sears, J. C. Penney and Montgomery Ward were watching, but they didn't realize just how fast the small chain was expanding until their catalogue sales began to suffer in the towns where he built a new store. They also didn't realize the change small-town America was experiencing. These customers were no different from their big-city counterparts in that they wanted the product, and they wanted it at the point of the sale.

Wal-Mart commanded the attention of Wall Street investors. The increases in the price of new Wal-Mart stock were very impressive. Sales were progressing at an unbelievable rate. The company showed $44 million in sales in

1970, compared to over \$1.8 billion by the end of the decade.

In order to realize his dream of an even larger Wal-Mart retailing operation, Walton knew he'd have to weed out his competition in the small towns where he wanted to expand. He knew he'd have to go head-to-head with the many small, established merchants who had served those communities for so many years. The major chains who were already vying for a spot in the small markets of middle America would have to be eliminated altogether. There simply wasn't room for more than one chain store in a small town.

Like a general in battle, Walton viewed his competitors as enemies, focusing on their weakest points. And he threw salt in those wounds whenever he could. To Walton, war was war, and the survivor would reap the benefits of a cornered market. Whenever Walton succeeded in killing off a competitor, he didn't burn any bridges with the locals. He often hired the upper management team from the failed store to work in his Wal-Mart outlet. And the people he hired were often the mayor, a member of the city council or of the school board. Walton dared not get them in a huff. Before he took over the retail market, he made peace by giving them first shot at an equal position in his new store. Walton could be very diplomatic when he had to be.

The tools of the Walton war machine were based on price. Walton didn't think twice about starting a price war in order to get the customer in the door. Even hardware stores, dress shops and drug stores that had long relied on the local customer for their survival fell by the wayside when the price war was on. Loyal customers, hurt by a fluctuating economy, lost their sense of loyalty when it came to the pocketbook. Walton was banking on this important factor. Even Walton was amazed at the success of the first 400 Wal-Marts since they had to compete with long-time merchants. He found out just where the buck stopped. So did most of his competition.

By the 1970s, Walton had the money and the resources to erase his competition through a massive buyout campaign. In 1977, he bought the 16 Mohr-Value stores in Missouri and Illinois and turned them into Wal-Mart outlets. This acquisition, Walton's first, was to be only the beginning in what would be an unprecedented expansion effort on the part of his mounting empire. No small chain would be safe from a Walton takeover effort. If he couldn't buy them out of business, he'd run them out of business.

At a time in the '70s when Americans were dealing with double-digit inflation, especially during the Jimmy Carter administration, Walton was actually prospering. During

1978, Wal-Mart expanded its trade territory to twenty-three states. Texas was the main market Sam wanted. Small states such as Iowa, Kansas, Louisiana and Mississippi, with small populations and many rural towns of 5,000 or less, became his other targets. He entered towns such as Monroe, Louisiana, McComb, Mississippi, and Waterloo, Iowa, remote regions where consumers previously had to drive over fifty miles to get the newest fashions or great buys on tires.

The company under Walton added fifty-four stores in 1979 alone. The competition was understandably nervous. Walton began zooming in on their territory, and they knew they'd have a hard time trying to fight him, one on one, in such a small market. Walton's need to expand was only exceeded by his need to dominate the retail market.

Walton decided his outlets were not utilizing their total square footage to maximum advantage. After he read that the Thompson brothers' 7-Eleven stores were the most profitable retail outlets per square foot in the world, he set out to find a way to go one step better.

The Hutchenson Shoe Company, a major seller of men's and women's footwear, known for leasing space in small department stores throughout the United States, was purchased by Walton in an effort to maximize his total sales. Many of the jewelry departments in the

Wal-Mart outlets were also acquired to assure his chain the greatest earnings in sales, rather than some outsider that was leasing space in the store. Throughout the years, he added automotive bays for car repairs and pharmacies to compete with the local drug store. He even began selling fish and birds and plants. If Walton thought it would sell, he stocked it. If it didn't, he'd get rid of it.

Saturation was the key idea in the late 1970s. Walton wanted to be the champion retailer in the breadbasket of America. His dividing lines were drawn, and he didn't bother with the east or west coast markets at that time.

The chain was massive. He opened an average of a hundred stores a year during the 1980s. Wal-Mart was now entering into areas once reserved for K-Mart and Sears, markets of 25,000 people or more, such as in Cedar Rapids, Iowa, Jackson, Mississippi, and even William Dillard's own backyard, Little Rock, Arkansas. No ground was safe from Sam's expansion. With all of middle America shopping at Wal-Mart, it's easy to see why Sam was beginning to tap the larger markets.

Even Walton's advertising, at one time found only in the local newspapers of rural middle America, was now appearing in every medium from *People* to *Time* magazine. And the Walton/Wal-Mart machine continued to roll over mid-America. He was putting an all-out effort into his expansion just as he had done building up his name. (He opened 54 stores in 1980, 161 in 1981, 60 in 1982, 91 in 1983, and 103 in 1984.) Walton continued to buy out the competition. In 1984, he made a deal to buy 92 Big-K stores and converted them into Wal-Mart look-alikes.

By 1988, Wal-Mart had grown to over 1,200 stores in 24 states, mostly in rural cities and towns. Distribution centers of 350,000 square feet were built in Searcy, Arkansas; Shreveport, Louisiana; Palestine, Texas; Cullman, Alabama; Mt. Pleasant, Iowa; Douglas, Georgia; Brookhaven, Mississippi; Laurens, South Carolina; New Braunfels, Texas; and Seymour, Indiana.

In 1977, Wal-Mart received its first national ranking by *Forbes* magazine in the publication's yearly "Forbes Yardsticks" column. The company was ranked first in the discount and variety stores division, overshadowing giants such as Sears and Montgomery Ward. Walton was elated. He went out and purchased an airplane to celebrate, one of only a handful of luxuries he ever bought for himself.

Wal-Mart was ranked first on return on equity and return of capital. It was also ranked first in sales and earning growth, all crucial to the sale of stock and future expansion.

Sam Walton was, in 1984, and for the first time, named the richest man in the United

States by the magazine, a label he despised intensely. Walton long had an undeclared war with *Forbes* over his personal wealth, but even he knew the figures were solid. When a reporter from a Washington newspaper came to Bentonville to interview Walton in light of the *Forbes* listing, he was directed to Walton's attorney. The reporter was curious if Mr. Walton was trying to hide something, maybe from the IRS. As usual, Walton's tight and loyal team sent the reporter on his way with little to go on. The only way to get to Walton was to work for him. After the *Forbes* report, Walton screened his upper management team personally.

The battle between Wal-Mart and K-Mart continued in the 1980s. With Wal-Mart at 1,300 stores and K-Mart at some 2,000, give or take a hundred, the race sped forward for the number two slot in American retailing. In 1990, Wal-Mart brought in $20 billion a year in gross sales, while K-Mart was hovering around $25 billion. Walton was closing in fast. In 1991, Wal-Mart finally succeeded in passing K-Mart. K-Mart stores lost ground because they are understaffed, understocked and have a cheap connotation to their product line. Even Johnny Carson and David Letterman get their jabs in on K-Mart, and their reputation is steadily going downhill. These television comedians also got their jabs in on Sam because of his wealth, but they tended to leave Wal-Mart out of the picture, since the chain has yet to enter the east or west coast markets.

7

The Reluctant Millionaire

In 1975, after Sam's wealth became common knowledge, politicians came courting. His potential was a topic of discussion for anyone wanting to run for public office in the state of Arkansas and on the national front. The movers and shakers around the world began to take notice of men like Walton. Their mounting wealth and hold on the various markets in which they operated made them prime targets for businessmen interested in middle America. From Taiwan to Japan and European countries, many were after Sam Walton. He was a target in the retail world.

In the Wal-Mart scheme of things, many employees were personally getting to know their boss by way of the escalating media attention Walton was receiving, not only from *Forbes*, but also from *Business Week*, *Time* and even

People magazine. They were curious as to his wealth. Nothing had been written on his life and his wealth. In fact, little was known about Sam Walton, where he came from and how he got so rich selling dry goods in small towns scattered throughout the nation. Oh, they had seen him come into a store and give one of his famous pep rallies to get them motivated for the day, but they didn't know just where the man came from and how he got to the exalted level he had reached in the retail world.

Dodging reporters became a new task for Walton. He even instigated a legal staff and a public relations staff to guide the media as they asked thousands of questions about his life and his family, an aspect of his life he deemed very private and none of anyone's business. Experts who followed his personal holdings in the company estimated his net worth by virtue of the company's growth and gross sales. Using those figures as a guideline, they were amazed at the rise of his personal wealth on a daily basis. But Walton continued to deny any out-of-this-world figures Americans were reading in their daily newspapers.

Walton initiated an effort to keep the press at bay. In 1978, when it was projected he would become a billionaire within the next three years, Walton put together a plan to reduce his profile in the company and became a reluctant millionaire in the public's eye. His best defense was remaining close to home and flying his small, private plane to store openings to avoid the press in public airports. This small plane gave Walton access to rural areas where a new store was to be dedicated. No one knew his itinerary, and therefore didn't know if he was coming or going. Whenever he saw the press, he ran. And he began to instruct all his store managers not to give out any information regarding his personal life, and praised his employees for complying with these instructions. In fact, he volunteered superficial information to many who sought to write about him and began a campaign of his own to put together his personal life story. Without the help of his staff and his family, an accurate portrait of his life couldn't have been written, mainly because Sam Walton was shy and embarrassed that anyone would want to write a book about his life. He was always under the impression everyone connected with the media wanted to hound him about his personal wealth. It's true his personal wealth was a main factor in his becoming a public figure in the first place, but his remarkable rise to the top of the retail world from such humble beginnings intrigued many members of the press even more.

Recreation for Sam Walton remained at the short end of a shotgun. From his childhood, he loved to hunt quail and dove, and with many of his upper management team, he'd fly to Texas to bag his limit.

He had an old hunting dog he loved and named Old Roy. This dog was dear to him and he took the hound on many a hunt. So attached to the dog was he that Walton worked with a dog food manufacturer and began selling dog food under the name "Old Roy," created for a fit and energetic canine. Helen wasn't much on hunting, but she went along on the trips with him, especially after the kids were grown, just to be with him. He had built a tennis court in his backyard and a swimming pool to keep his 5'8", 155-pound frame fit going into his fifth decade of life. He had been athletic all his life, and swimming was instrumental in keeping him fit. Sam always took care of himself. He was never one taken with drink and a billion-aire's nightlife. He was a family man with not a hint of personal scandal to blemish his life. He was always happy with Helen. They were cut from the same mold, and their love spanned many decades of dedication.

Those hunts down in Texas with Old Roy were some of the best times of his life. He lived for the serenity of a day-long hunt with friends and family. With the press dogging him better than Old Roy could dog a bird, he had to take his hunting trips in total secrecy. His manag-ers in Texas were instructed not to give out any information to anyone regarding the next hunt. They did so out of loyalty, not because they were in fear of losing their jobs. These managers really liked Sam Walton and were dedicated to him.

In the Wal-Mart stores, Sam made sure they had a well-stocked sporting goods department. Being the shy, unassuming man he was, he'd stand in line with the rest of the shoppers and pay cash for his shotgun shells. His love for hunting was only matched by his love of money and company success.

Sam didn't like the press dogging his family either. His oldest boy, Rob, a Yale graduate and his youngest son, Jim, lived in Bentonville and were constantly being called for interviews. Both boys became part of the company, and both learned to keep close-mouthed about their father's wealth. His brother, Bud, up until he moved to Alaska, also found it difficult to live in the small town, as the press knew just where to go to find them. Sam's daughter, Alice, continued to live in nearby Rogers, Arkansas, and she too found it difficult to keep the press away. Sam and his family received thousands of letters from poverty-stricken Americans after the *Forbes* list became public every October, and it was making it increasingly difficult for the entire family to remain out of the public's eye. They were bombarded with money requests for everything from braces for a little girl's teeth to tuition for a gifted mind to attend college. Even the PR staff was having difficulty keeping the cards and letters sorted.

As the family gained wealth, it began to take its toll on the Walton personal life. Sam and Helen's marriage was as solid as a rock, but the children were a different matter. Rob was divorced and then remarried with three children of his own, while Alice made two unsuccessful trips to the altar. Jim and John were holding their marriages together, but after the split of the stock in 1989, they too became billionaires, and it was becoming increasingly difficult to keep a focus on the family. John left Arkansas and opened a ship-building company in San Diego, California. Jim stayed on board in Bentonville, becoming president of Walton Enterprises, which takes care of the family's banks and property investments. Rob, armed with a law degree from Yale, became Chairman of Wal-Mart on his father's death. Alice accepted full responsibility for a tragic accident in 1989, when she struck and killed a pedestrian while driving to work. Alice was devastated but able to continue on. After her second divorce, she took $19 million of her Wal-Mart money and opened a company she called Llama Company, a combination broker-dealer, fixed portfolio management entity. She has a little of her father's drive in her, since she works sixty-hour weeks and owns a 900-acre cattle and horse farm on the side for relaxation. The divorces put distance between Sam and his oldest and youngest children, but they tried to keep awareness of the distance within the family.

During a class reunion in 1986, Sam relaxed a bit and allowed the citizens of Columbia to hound him a little. He signed autographs like a movie star and even gave a speech on his personal success story. His inability to cope with his wealth made him appear aloof and uncaring. But his personality kept him from facing a public determined to know intimate details of a public figure's lifestyle. Even Robin Leach, host of the television show "Lifestyles of the Rich and Famous," has never enticed Walton to appear on his show. Leach made a yearly request only to be politely turned down.

Reporters at the class reunion began to quiz Walton's classmates as to what Sammy Walton was like as a friend. Just as the loyal employees had, they declined to comment but gave the press the usual sugar-coated answers of greatness. Walton, who showed up in a polyester suit, off the rack, kept the press away from his side of the room. The Rolex watch he'd been given the Christmas before was absent. It seems he gave the watch away and bought a Timex. When asked why he didn't own a Rolls Royce, Walton replied, "My dogs don't like the smell of leather." He prefers to drive his two-year-old Ford pickup truck with the dent in the side. By keeping his profile that of the Average Joe, Walton continues to keep the press out of his very private life.

When 1980 rolled around, Wal-Mart was a retail machine squashing the competition. Its sales figures were likely keeping the boys over at Sears and K-Mart awake at night. Much to Walton's dismay, however, the press would not leave him alone. When he took a trip to Rio de Janeiro first class, the press made a big deal out of the fact he had never flown first class before, even though he could buy the entire airline. Any little thing he did made the personals column of the nations' newspapers. The *National Enquirer* as well as other supermarket tabloids began taking pictures of his house and interviewing local Bentonville citizens in their effort to learn more about Walton's personal life. With hopes of finding skeletons in his closet, they backed off when, as one rag put it, "there just wasn't anything there."

When he was described in the Thomas J. Peters and Roger H. Waterman book, *In Search Of Excellence*, he caught the attention of men and women in the business world who lived and worked outside the retail end. He was an odd man to many who read about him, and they thought him interesting.

The brokers of Wall Street found him to be the very life blood of the rise of Wal-Mart stock.

Whenever Walton had a good day, they wanted to know about it. He *was* Wal-Mart.

After his in-depth treatment in Nancy Austin's book, *A Passion For Excellence*, Walton became known to many who had never heard of him before. Even David Letterman and Johnny Carson were taking their shots at Walton's lifestyle in the hills of Arkansas. "Just who is this hermit in Arkansas named Sam Walton?" Letterman quipped in 1986. "Does he print his own money?"

The *Washington Post* reporter who traveled to Arkansas to get the real story of Sam Walton once and for all expected to find a fortress with servants and cars and opulence galore. He was amazed at how the richest man in America lived. He scoured Bentonville for a chance to talk to Walton but even the local barber who had been cutting Sam Walton's hair for nineteen years offered little help. The barber did tell the reporter about a time when Walton had left his wallet at home and insisted on returning to get it so he could pay for the haircut. The reporter left Bentonville with a story of how the richest man in America lives a simple, quiet life, preferring to stay away from the public that put him on top of the retail world.

"You go anywhere in the country, mention Bentonville, Arkansas, and they've heard of Sam Walton," Bill Fields, a local justice of the peace, offered the *Post* reporter. "He sure as hell didn't have to stay here after he made it." But he did, even after his home burned to the ground in the '70s from a lightning bolt striking the roofing shingles. Instead of building a grand mansion, he moved a double-wide trailer house on the property to keep his wealth out of the public eye as best he could. When Helen protested, he rebuilt the house on the same site, but this one was smaller since his kids were all grown. Helen, like Sam, enjoyed simple things, but living in a double-wide trailer was a little too simple for even Helen Walton.

The locals around Bentonville went the extra mile to help protect the billionaire's privacy. It was one of the strangest occurrences ever seen in modern rural living. Sam Walton was godlike to many; to others, he was a man deserving of privacy and they felt it was their job to help him out. Many locals work for Wal-Mart, and to add to their job security, they would offer very little about their connection with Walton. When he dropped into the coffee shop at the local Ramada Inn at 6 a.m. to have a light breakfast and read the morning paper, which he owned, Walton spoke very little to anyone.

Betty Robbins, a waitress who talked to Walton more than anyone on a daily basis while he was at his leisure, has put many a meddlesome reporter in his place. "It's personal," she replied when a reporter asked what Walton eats and who he talks to. "That's personal, too," she answered when asked if Walton tipped her well. It is known, just for the record, Walton ate a small breakfast of cereal and toast with coffee and juice. And he tipped in the twenty per cent range. Nothing fancy..It might have given him away. Tipping over twenty per cent in this part of the country would be downright patronizing. Arkansas people believe in getting paid what they're worth, nothing more and nothing less.

Walton's barber, John Mayhall, put it best when asked why Mr. Walton was such a reluctant millionaire.

"Mr. Sam isn't a front-page kind of guy," he said. "The day he finds his picture on the front page of a publication, he'll buy it and put the story to rest. Frankly, I wish they'd just leave him alone. He ain't like Donald Trump, always out to stroke his own ego. He's got too much class to be a Donald Trump."

8

Good-bye Mom and Pop America

When a man and woman open a business together, no matter how large or small, a certain amount of sentimental feeling goes along with it. There is a great satisfaction in being an entrepreneur. Many of the world's most successful couples in life as well as in business still can't describe the close bond that exists, even if the mom and pop operation grows into a billion-dollar industry.

From the beginning of the first merchants, many of whom were husband and wife teams, there has been something special about a mom and pop operation, no matter what type of business it is.

Sam and Helen Walton did not take the mom and pop route in business. Sam was the businessman and Helen the homemaker. In 1983, Helen did try her hand at retailing when she opened an arts and crafts store she called, appropriately, Helen's Arts and Crafts. The small chain grew to only three stores, but it proved Sam's success did indeed rub off a little. Helen's was sold to a larger chain of arts and crafts stores called Michael's in 1987, but not before she had made the business stand on its own.

Mom and pop America lived very well in rural areas as well in the cities of the United States. Many a couple opened delicatessens, grocery stores or laundries in the neighborhoods of America's cities, and they still thrive today. In small-town America, these couples were pillars of the communities they served. But there was a change taking place. People were buying their clothes and drugs and automotive needs where they could get the best price. The big merchants had the buying power to keep prices low and attract their customers from neighboring towns. Sam Walton knew if he could bring these prices to small-town America, he could succeed, even if it would all but wipe out mom and pop. It wasn't his initial intention, but he knew it was happening.

Retail outlets such as K-Mart and Wal-Mart became a new wind, blowing over small-town America in such a way as to overtake the day-to-day business customs of many of its residents. There was no way mom and pop could compete. In the early part of the 1950s, mom and pop didn't see it coming. To make a profit, they had to mark their products up to cover their costs. Walton and men like him had a wealth of buying power, and therefore they could do as they pleased in the small towns. By the 1960s, when loyalty went out the window in favor of low prices, mom and pop were wondering if they could survive.

When Walton opened a Wal-Mart store in a small town in Oklahoma in the mid-1970s, a little dress shop on the town square, which had enjoyed a healthy business for over forty years, had a low opinion of Walton's stock. The owners declared Walton couldn't compete with their quality. But what they didn't know is that even rural America was changing its buying habits. In the old days, a family bought school clothes, then either altered them as the children grew or handed them down to the next child in line. As peer pressure emerged, youngsters began demanding their own new clothes. Mom and pop didn't change fast enough, and children didn't want to shop where their parents had shopped as kids.

Wal-Marts, along with the huge mall down the road, were the places to be when it came to getting new clothes, records and bicycles.

And the prices. Walton and others like him could sell for pennies over the cost of the items and still make a handsome profit by the sheer numbers they sold every day. Mom and pop could not compete with such a setup.

A look at the small towns in America where Walton opened a Wal-Mart store will often reveal an empty town square. In these coves of Americana, the old businesses just could not match the newness of Sam's operation. They definitely couldn't match his price or selection, and thus closed. The town squares in many hundreds of these small cities became nothing more than relics. Some became partial ghost towns when the merchants moved to strip centers near the Wal-Mart store, in an effort to get the overflow. The dress shops, drug stores, Western Autos, OTASCOS, and even jewelry stores are all but gone. Springhill, Louisiana, Atoka, Oklahoma, Pleasanton, Texas, McComb, Mississippi, and even Walton's hometown of Columbia, Missouri, are reeling from the crunch. Mom and pop will soon be a thing of the past.

Dowdy's Men's and Boys' Wear is a prime example of a mom and pop operation, handed down over many generations, which has yet to buckle under to the local Wal-Mart. Owned and operated by the Dowdy family of Pleasanton, Texas, it sells quality western wear, hats, boots and suits and has for over forty years. And it has made the Dowdy family somewhat wealthy in its own right. When Sam opened a Wal-Mart outlet in Pleasanton in 1986, Mom and Pop Dowdy knew they were in for a fight, but the town council gave Walton his normal concessions of tax waivers and utility hookups at a discounted price in the hopes of obtaining the hundred jobs Walton promised the community. Wal-Mart has lived up to its word of providing the jobs, but the cities of Pleasanton and neighboring Jourdanton are now paying the price. The tax waivers bought jobs but put a lasting strain on the old shops that had been in business for years. Many were wondering if it was all worth it. With the addition of some 20,000 square feet and a new automotive center, other local merchants are now worrying right along with them.

Walton's buying power closed six mom and pop operations in five years in the Pleasanton area. Although Dowdy's remains intact, the practice of selling the same jeans at three dollars over Wal-Mart's price is a clear danger. Dowdy has deep pockets and has the ability to carve an old and established clientele out of the many who are set in their ways. Cities all across America, with thousands of mom and pop operations which thrived for decades, changed as Walton opened more and more stores.

New Braunfels, Texas, a medium-sized city with an attractive tourist trade, is home to a Wal-mart store and a K-Mart outlet. These two outlets have made the downtown area a virtual ghost town. The city even hired a consultant to revitalize the area, and those shops remaining in the downtown sector banded together to fight Walton to the end.

Jacksonville, Texas, Hattiesburg, Mississippi, Magnolia, Arkansas, and Ardmore, Oklahoma, are just a few of the cities where the town council stopped to rethink its position regarding the concessions it gave Walton to open one of his stores. Many of the old-timers, the mom and pops of the nation, were fighting mad at the thought of Walton getting a tax break just to go into business under their noses. But a weakened economy, brought on by the increased need for jobs, put mom and pop between a rock and a hard place.

One of the saddest things a mom and pop operation must face is the closing of a lifelong retail outlet. It's true that if it hadn't been Sam Walton, it would have been some other retail giant, but that doesn't ease the pain. And the entire community feels it. The local mom and pop merchants were assets to the community, often opening up on a given moment just to keep the business and help out a neighbor in need. But mom and pop have always been slow to change, in stock or in price or when it came to dealing with competition. Competition is going to happen as we enter a newer, faster age. Those neglecting to move right alongside these retailers will most definitely be left behind.

The closings happened every day as Walton continued to expand into rural and urban areas of the nation. And when those people were forced out of business, they usually wound up working for the very man who did them in: Sam Walton. Expertise in their fields made them ideal candidates for the new jobs. Walton won on all fronts. He got new employees with a wealth of knowledge, men who owned gun shops for his sporting goods department, women who owned dress shops for his ladies wear and those who used to work for them who were then unemployed. They became part of the Wal-Mart team. And he got them at minimum wage. A hard aspect is that many of the defeated had to answer to the very man who put them out of a business they may have been a part of since their grandparents opened up many years ago.

In reality, how could mom and pop compete? A local merchant who had a hardware store in El Dorado, Arkansas, was selling rakes for $7.98 each. Walton came to town and sold the very same rake for $4.98, and in three sizes with different colors. A customer's pocketbook knows no loyalty when it comes to saving money, as well it shouldn't. Times are tough all over, and looking for the best buy is and always has been a consumer tradition.

That is the heart of the reason why mom and pop failed to keep up with men like Walton.

They are set in their ways. This subtle stubbornness could very well mark their demise. Just as times change, so does everything within it. Mom and pop used to be the heart of retailing in America. Today, they are quickly becoming dinosaurs.

Richard Lingeman, the author of a book entitled *Small Town America*, touches on this very important point of why men like Walton are putting urban-like buying into rural settings. He tells of a day when mom and pop America will be nothing more than a memory and of how big-time retail outlets will serve even the most remote areas of the nation's needs. He points out that in the old small town America, everyone knew who everyone else was and what they did for a living. They knew the druggist and the grocer and the mechanic. Today, people don't even know their next-door neighbor. That is where this country has evolved, and it's no wonder why a Wal-Mart can thrive so well in a rural environment as well as an urban setting. Many of the cities who fought giving Walton any concessions at all still saw their downtown areas become vacant.

Just as the neighborhood cafe laughed at the thought of a man opening a hamburger joint with golden arches and a clown out front, never thinking for a moment people would actually be so busy they would take a meal and drive off, so did the mom and pop operations Walton throttled while building his empire. No one is laughing now, especially the mom and pop operations that folded under the strain of the innovative Wal-Mart down the street.

Small-town merchants have sometimes boasted that they've fought off big city merchants for decades. What they didn't realize was that the drive into the city is now only around the corner for all the customers they had served. They have also said Sam Walton couldn't compete, given Walton's poor quality of merchandise.

In this give and take society, with a divorce rate of fifty percent, men and women rebuilding their lives with kids in tow aren't looking for that thousand-dollar bedroom suite to last a lifetime, because a lifetime today ain't what it used to be. " 'Til death do us part" is sometimes over in an instant. Walton's furniture will do just fine for the moment.

"Wal-Mart is not in the business to suck dollars away from the local economy, but to enrich the community," said the manager of the Georgetown Wal-Mart. Chief among the people enriched was Sam Walton, but there is nothing wrong with a little old-fashioned free enterprise. Those who build the better mouse-trap have always enjoyed the riches afforded their efforts.

Oh, that downtown coordinator hired to revitalize the square in New Braunfels, Texas, told the city council it could take two or three years to achieve their goals, instead of the projected one year. Meanwhile, Sam Walton began an expansion effort so great, those two or three years would no doubt turn into four or five, then six or seven and so on. You either have it or you don't. The downtown merchants of small-town America no longer possess the very essence of competition: low prices. Sam Walton was the master of the price war. Mom and pop America are simply outnumbered, literally.

Mom and pop merchants are a dying breed. They just don't know it yet. As Sears, Wal-Mart and K-Mart fight it out for the top spot in retailing, mom and pop will be caught in the middle, and they simply don't have the resources to come out of the battle alive. Logically, no one has deeper pockets than the richest man in America, should he decide to run mom and pop out of business on his own. Instead, he did it methodically, from behind the scenes in the continuing war with his two top rivals. But it was not with hatred. It was just free enterprise to the letter, the way Sam Walton invented it from scratch. Mom and pop enjoyed it for many, many decades. With the changing times, others like Walton are now enjoying it.

Any mom and pop store that thought it could go head to head with Walton was sadly mistaken. It may very well have survived for a while, but as the retail world changed, so did

America's buying habits. America will forget the mom and pop merchant, just as it has forgotten the horse and buggy and the kerosene lamp. They worked well for the time, but the times are definitely changing. Just as the videotape will replace the theaters of the nations, and the fax machine will replace the U.S. Postal Service, so will Sam Walton's retail machine replace the mom and pop merchants as it rolls across America into the 1990s. Those who realize that change is inevitable can be the next Sam Walton of the twenty-first century.

9

Changing Times in Direct Competition

Edward Brennan, CEO of industry leader Sears, Roebuck & Company, and Joseph Antonio, head man at K-Mart, had a problem: how did you deal with Sam Walton and Wal-Mart going into the 1990s? With the growth of Wal-Mart, number three in the retail world and climbing daily, it would be up to them to keep their respective positions in the retail scheme of things. Frankly, they had their jobs cut out for them.

Sam Walton, even when he was no longer working on a daily basis, had laid out a plan so tight that it was only a matter of time before both of them would fall.

K-Mart was a store chain under siege and had been for the past ten years. The stores are larger than those of Wal-Mart, with some 75,000 to 90,000 square feet, mainly centered in cities of at least 20,000 residents. K-Mart carved out a niche for itself during the early days of Wal-Mart's expansion, preferring to leave small-town America to Walton and the mom and pop operations. Now that mom and pop were almost extinct, K-Mart was next on the list. Sam Walton was in the position to take on his competition on both ends of the spectrum. He edged his way into both arenas by going head-to-head with their markets, methodically beating them at every turn.

Antonio and K-Mart didn't take Wal-Mart and Walton seriously ten years ago. But Joseph Antonio's store had an image problem. Television comedians were making fun of K-Mart as a low-income chain with its "blue light" specials. The product line which once made K-Mart the leader in small discount stores throughout the United States was now sub-standard to the American shopper. Consumers wanted quality as well as quantity and they wanted friendlier service, something K-Mart lacked. K-Mart stores were getting dirtier, with popcorn on the dingy floors, and poorly stocked shelves made the customer think twice about shopping there.

Walton, on the other hand, saw these seemingly frivolous weaknesses and worked on them. His "Letter to the President" campaign, an effort put together by Walton personally to get feedback from his customers, worked. And he took their compliments and complaints to heart and made sure his managers did too. Antonio was lagging far behind in customer satisfaction.

In an effort to end the "polyester" line of clothing that was so much a part of K-Mart's reputation, Antonio introduced a Jaclyn Smith line of shirts and pants, and called upon upscale caterer Martha Stewart to advertise K-Mart as being more than just a store that sells can openers and car stereos. With Wal-Mart nipping at his heels, Antonio reportedly spent many hours of his work week searching for big names to join the ranks in his battle against Sam Walton. He claimed the chain would always "keep a promotional feel to their sales effort" but the battle was already being waged for the top spot, and Walton had the inside track. Attention K-Mart employees: beware of the Wal-Mart down the street. You might be working there in the 1990s.

Sears Roebuck was the nation's largest retail outlet in the 1980s, twice the size of K-Mart and three times larger than Wal-Mart. But Edward Brennan was feeling the impact of Sam Walton's hold on retail sales in America. In 1989, for the first time in its 102-year history, Sears closed its doors for three days to reprice and rethink its place in the retail world. And it didn't look good. Sears was big and bulky and old-fashioned. The stores were built when families shopped together and made a day of it. Now, in America's fast-paced society with the competition of discount stores such as Wal-Mart, Sears outlets were out of touch with the times. They were losing money when they should have been changing and expanding to meet the needs of an ever-changing buying public.

For the Christmas rush of 1987, Sears sales rose 4.9 percent. K-Mart increased 8.0 percent and J. C. Penney, another dinosaur, reported 8.6 percent. Wal-Mart, on the other hand, rose a whopping 34 percent. Each and every year since 1987, Wal-Mart has outsold its competitors, again and again. At a time of the year when retail sales should be at their best and the stores behind them should be realizing a greater profit margin, only Wal-Mart could boast remarkable growth.

In 1989, Sears contemplated moving out of Chicago. It also cut eight hundred jobs in a further move to lower the cost of doing business. Regional offices of the company took the brunt of the layoffs. In Texas, the Houston office was closed and the Dallas location was trimmed to the bone. But the price restructuring plan which closed the company's doors for a few days wasn't working either. Public opinion revealed people didn't think the newest changes would alter their spending habits one bit.

Sears, like K-Mart, has suffered somewhat because of appearance and employee apathy. Service and a pleasant atmosphere were two ingredients that built these two chains. When you begin to compromise these main business factors, people tend to change right along and start spending their money with the new kid on the block. That new kid in the 1960s and the 1970s was Sam Walton.

Brennan was also examining Sears's other holdings, such as Dean Witter Reynolds investment offices and Coldwell Banker real estate outlets. He wanted to return to the things that made the company great—selling merchandise. Sears had entered an area of offering services in areas it wasn't schooled in. It was too little, too late. Brennan even began a campaign to advise the public it too has "everyday low prices." The public, however, knows better. Sears remains somewhat overpriced on many items Wal-Mart sells extremely cheaply every day. Sears had yet to learn that getting into a price war with Wal-Mart was detrimental to its existence. With its rural outlets, Wal-Mart would win by virtue of its location in those areas. Sears forgot the high cost of gasoline in the 1970s which also contributed to its downfall in the retail world. Sam Walton didn't forget—and outside influences such as high gas prices, war, crime, etc., were all factors in the location of his outlets.

Walton devised a plan to become number one in the retail world by 1995, and there was nothing Walton liked better than going head-to-head with the competition on a direct course of battle. He could compete with the best of them on price, but his strategy was not price alone. It was good old-fashioned service. Sam Walton instructed his troops to do one important thing while they plowed their way to the top: fight Sears and K-Mart in their own backyards.

In 1988, Wal-Mart, known for keeping its distance from urban areas and widely known for spending little on national advertising, changed its tune. David Glass, with Mr. Sam's blessing, targeted Sears and K-Mart in the larger cities of Dallas, St. Louis, Orlando, Atlanta, Denver and Nashville to fight them on their own turf.

Adding even more power to the fight, Glass initiated an enormous advertising campaign to inform consumers that Wal-Mart was coming to the big city. In national publications such as *People* magazine and *Parade*, the newspaper supplement, as well as on television, the many old Wal-Mart customers who had moved away from the rural stores and still "wanted their Wal-Mart" were targeted to receive the letter. No one knew the Wal-Mart customer better than Walton. He realized many had moved to the city. And he was now willing to move with them.

In 1988, Sam opened three Wal-Marts in Austin, Texas, each with 90,000 square feet or more, perfectly positioned and easily accessible. Sales for Sears and K-Mart dropped dramatically—so much so that the two giants had to revamp their stores physically to make a visible change to their operations. Walton was keeping the heat on and keeping the competition on the run. With the ability to open two hundred stores annually while K-Mart hovered around fifty, Walton realized his dream of being number one in 1991, four years before his 1995 goal.

By 1990, Wal-Mart had bought out the 21 D. H. Holmes department stores operating in the southern region of middle America, as part of its larger-city expansion. New Orleans was the main reason for the buyout, as Holmes is an old and established name in that area. It was the first time Wal-Mart entered into such a large market, having remained historically in small Louisiana cities such as Lafayette and Houma.

Fortune magazine's survey of the best firms in the United States consistently put Wal-Mart at the top of the list of companies that perform better than their competition. As the times change, Wal-Mart continued to weed out its foes without fancy gimmicks or compromises. The company was in an ideal situation in the marketplace to eliminate its competitors. Any company that is unwilling to see the changing customer will be unable to embrace the adjustments needed within its operation. They will also become dinosaurs going into the next century. In order to run with the pack, the retail giants will have to keep up with the times by listening to their customers and watching their buying habits.

As this book goes to press, Wal-Mart has 1,718 stores—with more opening all the time.

10

Forbes Digs a Goldmine

A popular feature of *Forbes* magazine for more than ten years has been the "400 Richest Americans" list. Sam Walton topped that list for five consecutive years.

Instead of reporting on Walton's latest acquisitions, *Forbes* preferred to report where the money came from and in what quantity. Americans were asking about Sam Walton, who he was and what made him so rich. *Forbes* magazine provided the inside information on the wealthiest Americans to appease an ever-increasing appetite from its readers.

When Sam Walton entered the list at number two in the nation in 1984, few had ever heard of him. His low profile and easy-going ways never captivated the business world. He was the silent giant coming over the horizon. Wall Street knew who he was and of the great strides the small retailer was making against his competition. They were aware that his stock was strong on the market, but until the *Forbes* list, they had no idea of the vast personal wealth of the man behind the machine.

In 1984 Walton grew uncomfortable with the magazine's publication of a part of his life he considered extremely private. It would mark the beginning of a personal war against *Forbes* magazine that Sam Walton would eventually lose. He became impatient and instructed his staff to do all it could to stifle the publicity the list was generating.

In 1985, Sam was given the top spot with an estimated net wealth of some $2.8 billion. Wal-Mart sales were at an all-time high of $8.5 billion, and Walton held on to 39 per cent of the company.

Henry Ross Perot of Dallas came in at $1.8 billion while David Packard of Los Altos, California, was listed at $1.3 billion.

Once the news of this unknown man named Sam Walton came out for the first time at the top of the list, there was a mad scramble to find him. Bentonville, Arkansas, is tucked away in the corner of the state and difficult to reach. Reporters from around the nation were booking flights into Little Rock, then taking a commuter flight into Fayetteville, then renting a car and driving the twenty-five miles into Bentonville.

When they began to arrive, Sam instructed his staff to present them only with information about the company. They were not to give anyone information of his whereabouts, his family's lifestyle or their position. One day Walton was cornered at the Daylight Doughnut Shop on the main street in Bentonville by a *New York Times* reporter who found him at five in the morning drinking coffee and reading the local newspaper. The reporter asked him what he thought about being named the richest man in the nation on the *Forbes* 400 list.

"Oh, that damn list . . . I wish they'd just bury the thing and get it over with . . . I'm not that rich anyway, it's all paper, just paper," Walton responded.

When Walton's name continued to appear at the top of the list year after year, the calls kept coming in. Every year the list hit the racks, Phil Donahue put his call in for an interview on national television. And every year Walton declined.

In 1987, Walton was listed at a wealth of $4.5 billion. John Kluge of Metromedia had replaced Perot at $3.5 billion, and Perot fell to number three at $3 billion after selling his share of Electronic Data Systems to General Motors. Packard was fourth at $2.5 billion. To attract young readers, *Forbes* began a Top 40 highest paid entertainers list. In 1988, with his acquisition of the Beatles' Northern Songs catalogue, Michael Jackson came in first with $97 million. Actor Bill Cosby, who was selling books on the side at an alarming rate, placed second at $92 million, while movie director Steven Spielberg was listed at $64 million. From Sylvester Stallone to Oprah Winfrey, from Prince, Sting and Van Halen to Wayne Newton and Frank Sinatra, the list gave the public a sense of just how much money was floating around in the stars' heads. With all their riches, Sam Walton had made more money than all of them put together. His personal wealth and holdings were mind-boggling. Never before in the history of the United States were there so many billionaires at one time. And Sam Walton's personal position at the top of that list made him one of the richest men in the world.

T. Boone Pickens, Donald Trump and Al Copeland of Popeye's Famous Fried Chicken fame were constantly listed on *Forbes* 400 Richest Americans. These men wanted to be listed. They liked the rankings because it enhanced their business position in their respective endeavors.

Walton, on the other hand, was tired of the letters and phone calls from desperate Americans wanting him to buy them something. He was also increasingly fearful of kidnappers and threats and instructed his staff to take anything out of the ordinary very seriously.

Much like Howard Hughes before him, Walton was becoming paranoid, and not without good reason. A man had threatened to kidnap one of Sam's grandchildren to get a piece of the Walton pie. Nothing ever came of it, but the threat was made, and there was no guarantee it wouldn't happen again. Sam instructed his children to hire security to protect themselves and their families. "Be on the lookout," he told them.

Fortune magazine, not to be outdone by rival *Forbes*, instigated a new list of the world's billionaires. At the top of the twenty-five names was Sultan Hassanal Bolkiah, 41, of Bendar Seri Begawan, Brunei. He was listed as having an estimated personal wealth of at least $25 billion. A staggering amount by any means. Second on the list was King Fahd, 67, of Riyadh, Saudi Arabia. His wealth was put at some $20 billion. Then came Sam Walton, 69, of Bentonville, Arkansas, with $8.9 billion followed by Queen Elizabeth, 61, of London, England, at $7.4 billion. Twelve of the top twenty-five were from the United States.

Then came *Forbes* with a list of its own. By now it was becoming a game of who was right and who was wrong. *Forbes* magazine listed a Japanese real estate tycoon named Yoshiaki Tsutsumi as the world's richest man at $18.5 billion, with Sam Walton coming in at a paltry seventh place with his $8.5 billion.

The public didn't know who was reporting the world's richest people correctly. What they did know, however, was that Sam Walton was the wealthiest man in the United States with no sign of letting up. Only Walton held the key to getting his name off the list.

By late 1988, at the age of 70, Walton seriously considered passing the wealth along to his children. A victim of leukemia, then in remission, Walton was generally rethinking his life. Walton, who often wondered why his brother left Arkansas for Venezuela, Alaska, and the high seas, began to think it wasn't such a bad idea to get away from it all and live a little.

Helen concurred. The many trips they had taken to Texas, hunting quail, seemed not enough for Walton.

In October 1989, Sam decided to remove his name from the *Forbes* list. With almost nine billion dollars in personal wealth, he believed it was time to give the children their inheritance. Rob, John, Jim and Alice all received $1.8 billion from the split and instantly became four of the wealthiest Americans alive. John W. Kluge took over the top spot on the list with $5.2 billion, and Sam fell somewhere between tenth and fifteenth on the list. *Forbes* had contemplated for many years since instigating the list how a family fortune should be viewed. At what point does actual control of the family fortune pass from parent to child, and therefore at what point should the family's wealth be realigned? Sam made it easy for *Forbes* to change its list.

At age 71, he clearly became less active in the company. He relinquished the job of chief executive officer and remained chairman of the board.

The children, all active adults in their forties with professional interests and families of their own, began taking a increasing role in the investment decisions for the family holding company. Even the holding company itself was reorganized from the family corporation set up in 1969, to a straightforward partnership, with each of Sam's four children full and equal partners. The mantle had begun to pass in Bentonville, Arkansas. And the split to a partnership would avoid double taxation on dividends.

11

A Run for the Hills

Sam once said that if he didn't enjoy working, he'd "run off to Florida or Australia, get away from it all like my brother did." Instead, Walton chose to stay in the hills of Arkansas, playing tennis, swimming and hunting in season. He lived a quiet life, but the increasing position of Wal-Mart and the constant public image he was forced to deal with made Walton a man on the run. People were intrigued with the man who lived like a hermit in the hills of Arkansas.

Sam still made public appearances when a Wal-Mart outlet opened. But once the stores began to be situated in high-profile areas with larger markets, Walton grew skeptical about attending. When he did, he flew his small plane personally with a couple of friends from Bentonville.

Walton's resistance to being in the public eye extended to other areas where he was called upon to be the main focus of an event. He started receiving personal awards. In 1978 he was named "Man of the Year" by *Retail Week Magazine*, and "Discounter of the Year" by *Discount Store News*. In 1980, Sam was inducted into the Discounting Hall of Fame. In 1984, he received the Horatio Alger Award.

That year, he also received an honorary doctorate degree from the University of Arkansas. Walton made a short speech and sped away.

In 1983, the entire town of Bentonville, and governors and senators of every state where Walton sells his wares, paid tribute to the man who employed tens of thousands of American citizens, in a day hailed as "Sam and Helen Walton Appreciation Day." A phone call from then–President Reagan highlighted the evening.

When *Financial World* named Walton its 1985 CEO of the Year, Walton was downright embarrassed.

"I couldn't have done anything without the people that run those stores on a day-to-day basis," he said in accepting the honor. "They are the ones who deserve all the credit."

Sam also got a few awards he didn't care for. His quiet, simple lifestyle in the hills of Arkansas was the brunt of many jokes throughout the United States by comedians such as Johnny Carson and David Letterman. In 1987, he shared an award with Letterman from the International Dull Folks as being one of the dullest Americans. Ann Landers, TV anchor Tom Brokaw, Joan Rivers and Robin Leach were also on the list.

His life, and that of others, was becoming a circus side show. Whenever the press couldn't get to Walton, it seemed they tried to put him down. With the people Walton had around him, keeping all members of the press at bay, innuendo and hearsay were fast becoming the only basis for writing about him.

Sam continued his quiet lifestyle. He kept on driving his old Ford truck, and occasionally he'd use his 1976 Chevrolet Impala to "keep the battery up." His low profile, however, didn't keep him out of the business community, a place where he felt more comfortable. He was on the board of directors of Winn-Dixie Stores, Inc., of Jacksonville, Florida. As owner of the bank of Bentonville, the Bank of Rogers, Arkansas, and the Bank of Pea Ridge, Arkansas, Walton didn't mind the higher profile. Also, having Charles Lazarus, chairman of the board of Toys "R" Us, Inc., and James H. Jones, CEO of Jameson Pharmaceutical, on the Wal-Mart Board of Directors with the Walton family did nothing but keep his name on the tongues of business professionals throughout the nation, even though Walton rarely left his hometown.

But the press continued to try and dig its way into his life. Whenever he attended a University of Arkansas football game in nearby Fayetteville, the press would show up in hopes of getting an interview on his next great business move. Walton was a mover and shaker who didn't want any part of it. As Wal-Mart moved into the larger cities of the nation, Walton couldn't have picked a better time to run for the hills.

Rob Walton took up the slack. A bicyclist who raced in competition at age 45, Rob keeps a higher profile than his father. Brother Jim, president of Walton Enterprises, is an architecture buff who leads the press on his many restoration projects. They handle the press better than their father did.

In the early days of his wealth, Sam shrugged off the press and failed to deal with them, giving them the fuel they needed to think he might have something to hide. Rob and Jim face the press and learned to let them in on certain aspects of their personal lives. John, the middle boy, stays away from it all in San Diego, California.

12

The Meat Behind the Potatoes

When evaluating a company's position in the marketplace, business publications study certain areas. They want to determine what makes the company tick, what is the substance of the company, what keeps it in the public eye and how it reached the position it presently holds.

In the initial days of Wal-Mart, it was Sam Walton himself who accomplished these feats. He was the meat behind the potatoes, and through his guidance, Wal-Mart is the all-American success story. With a team that thinks as Sam thought, the future looks bright.

David D. Glass, the current president, kept his position when Rob Walton took over as chairman after his father's death. Men like Glass, who has been with Wal-Mart since 1976 and helped build the company, are the very reason Walton succeeded in business through constant changes in the retail world. Looking down the list of each and every member of upper management, Walton not only formed the company, he also formed the staff in his own image.

The main ingredient to the success of Wal-Mart and Sam's position as its founder has to be the down-home service. Even though prices are the mainstay, Walton's indoctrination of his people to be themselves while they sell merchandise was a success story within itself.

What made Wal-Mart one of the top companies in the world in such a short time? Presently, Wal-Mart ranks ahead of such companies as Coca-Cola, Chevron and rival Sears, in stock market value. In percentage change from one year to the next based on company growth, Wal-Mart is the number one company in the world, overshadowing such giants as IBM, Exxon, AT&T, GM and Ford. By 1995, Wal-Mart will be the darling of the stock market in terms of blue chip stocks. There are employees who are millionaires by virtue of the stock they hold.

One of the dumbest things I have ever done as a kid working for Wal-Mart was to decline to buy into a stock option. Stock bought in the early days has increased more than any other stock on the board.

The initial offering of 100 shares in 1970 was $1,650. After seven splits, those shares are now worth a whopping one-half million dollars. Who ever said a college student was smart?

A personal touch is the key to the company's success on a daily basis. Walton had his finger on the pulse of the customer as well as on his employees. His "Letter to the President" program, which gave his employees a chance to get a word in edgewise, was one of the most successful feedback programs in business. He listened to what they had to say, and by doing so helped curb pilfering, shoplifting and employee gripes. David Glass is continuing the tradition.

The new, aggressive move into the urban areas, along with an intensive ad campaign, is making Wal-Mart known on both the east and west coasts. These moves will provide the foundation for a truly national sales base.

In order to compete, Wal-Marts included pharmacies, nurseries and a complete automotive workplace for major repairs. When Walton only operated in small-town America, these—and, of course, prices—were the main elements which attracted customers from their long-time loyalties. Moving into the larger markets, head-to-head with Sears and K-Mart, Walton knew price wouldn't be the only factor. Service would run them out of business because they lacked the personal touch. Looking back, those in-store "pep rallies" Walton used to hold on a regular basis became valid. He knew what he was doing right from the start.

One night, when he couldn't sleep, Walton went to an all-night bakery and bought two dozen doughnuts for the boys at the loading dock on the night shift. He asked them what they thought the company was doing right and what should be changed. When he learned they needed two more showers in the men's locker room, that it was taking a man too long to get cleaned up before he went home at night, Walton had two showers installed the next day.

Sam Walton was a man of his word, and taking care of business on a regular basis was job one. When all is said and done, Sam Walton's conservative ways, his hands-on approach to any problem, customer or employee, were the true meat behind the potatoes.

When the unions put a move on Walton, he lashed out. He believed such organizations were a necessity in the early part of the century. In today's society, however, with so many companies overseas competing for a share of the American pie, he saw unions as the dinosaurs of the future, which had no place in the modern marketplace. It's every man for himself. Those who build the better mousetrap are the ones who should reap the rewards of free enterprise.

Playing With the Big Boys

13

Relentless Low Profile

Handing over the reins in 1988 to David Glass was not the corporate shake-up the business world was led to believe by the press. Sam Walton, after his leukemia was in remission, found himself re-evaluating his life, both business and personal. His business change was set forth by his own admission that after some thirty-five years of fourteen-hour days, it was time to slow down. His replacement, David Glass, had worked under Walton for over twelve years. He, even better than Rob or Bud Walton, knew what Sam wanted for the company's future and what direction to take. In Sam's life there were two situations where the man was at a loss for words: when his beloved hunting dog, Old Roy, died in 1982 and the day he decided to leave his Wal-Mart presidency.

With the help of Helen, Sam knew the time was right to retire. He also knew that handing over the reins meant a lower profile for him, from the public, the competition and the press.

Walton never quite succeeded in creating a sympathetic image for the press. Instead of stopping for reporters to answer any and all questions, Walton ran, thinking it a necessity to keep his profile out of the public entirely. What Walton needed was a good public relations man. He thought he had one in his general counsel and secretary, Robert K. Rhoads.

Rhoads was a legal man, not a PR man. His idea of helping Walton's image of great personal wealth was shallow and uninspiring, to say the least. Walton put the public relations job in Rhoads's hands, letting him talk to the public and the press any way he saw fit, as long as he and Helen and the children were not disturbed.

To keep his name out of the public eye, Sam did little to accommodate the press. The divorces of his children didn't make national headlines but, on the state-wide level, they were big topics of discussion. He was still standing in line buying his shotgun shells and flying his Piper Aztec around the nation to oversee his Wal-Mart operations, but he was careful not to rock the boat and allow the press to enter his life. Bentonville, Arkansas, was the perfect place to hide.

14

To Do as the Americans Do?

Keeping American dollars in America has been a challenge for every administration since the turn of the century. With the technology in Japan and Germany, and the cheap labor in Asian countries and Mexico, Americans have been in a cold trade war since the end of World War II.

Sam Walton perceived the trend in 1978, when he saw Chrysler decline and be surpassed by foreign auto makers. There was a direct link to a rising problem, and Walton wanted to do something about it. A public effort from Walton and his Wal-Mart chain would look good to the customer and give the image of an all-American place to shop for American-made goods. After the fall of Chrysler, many people began to rethink just where their goods were made. Price was becoming less important in the face of failing companies and rising unemployment.

Bob Hope, among others, went on national TV to encourage the American people to buy American-made goods and services. By doing so, and with his all-American image, Hope was once again campaigning for the American cause in much the same way he'd done during the wars in which he entertained troops. After the series of commercials by Hope, the American people began to look upon Japan and others more as the enemy once again, but this time in a business sense. Companies like Chrysler, Wal-Mart and Sears jumped on the bandwagon.

Lee Iacocca went on national TV to tell the American people that buying American-made cars and trucks was the only way to keep jobs in America. Just when Japan was making headway in the vital American marketplace, it was halted in part by Hope and Iacocca. During the Reagan administration, it was once again popular—with the Vietnam wounds beginning to heal—to wave the flag and be an American.

In an effort to illustrate the American way of doing business, and with a new leader in Moscow, Sam Walton, Democratic Arkansas Senator David Pryor and nine other business-men traveled to the Soviet Union in March 1988. Their goal was to speak with Mikhail Gorbachev about world trade and the possibil-ity of opening up the Soviet Union to western goods. Walton planned to tell the Soviet leader that goods and services would be beneficial to his people, and trading with the United States was the wave of the future. Although the delegation failed to gain an audience with Gorbachev, they met with many business leaders and exchanged ideas on world trade. By 1989, with glasnost in place, the future appeared promising for American companies wanting to do business in the USSR. One day, beside the Kentucky Fried Chicken stand, there may be a Wal-Mart going head-to-head with a Sears, Roebuck and Company.

On March 15, 1985, Sam sent a message to his merchandise managers.

"Find products that American manufacturers have stopped producing because they couldn't compete with foreign imports," Walton instructed. This mandate was the result of Walton's concern for the economy's high balance of trade deficits and the growing loss of jobs and dollars flowing out of America and into the hands of unfair trade partners such as Japan and Korea. That concern was translated in a letter to Wal-Mart's 3,000 domestic suppliers stating that between 1981 and 1984 an estimated 1.6 million American jobs were lost to imports. In one year, 1983–1984, non–oil related imports grew to $70 billion, a 33 per cent increase, while the balance of the trade deficit grew by 78 per cent, to $123.3 billion.

And the solution to the problem looked grim.

"Something can and must be done to reverse this very serious threat to our free enterprise system," Walton said. Although he was aware of the problem, he was apparently unwilling to step out and take a stand. Wal-Mart stores were buying foreign goods in record quantities to keep prices low enough to fight the rising competition in the American retail world. He also knew he'd have to make public appearances to become a champion of the cause and lead the way. Guarding his privacy, he chose not to take the initiative.

Wal-Mart established the "Buy American" program anyway in the summer of 1985. It was designed to work toward a long-range goal of strengthening the free enterprise system.

It was not intended to be an anti-import campaign. At Wal-Mart it couldn't have been. Walton had rice boxes stacked to the top of his warehouses throughout the United States, since price was still the number one consideration. But when he could, if the price was competitive, Walton instructed his buyers to get the products from American businesses. With cheap labor overseas, Walton bought very few American goods in addition to his current purchases.

The "Buy American" program looked good on paper, but no company in the United States that had to compete in the ever-changing American marketplace could afford to be part of the program on a large scale. "Buy American" was also intended to be a cooperative effort between retailers and domestic manufacturers to re-establish a competitive position in price and quality of American-made goods. The gap between retail and manufacturers widened every year once Japan and other nations were allowed to do business with the United States after World War II.

To bring the program to the front of American retailing, Walton put together a personal campaign for Wal-Mart that would make it appear to be a leader in the "Buy American" program. Whenever he made a deal with an American supplier of goods, he'd let the business community know in detail what transpired. Walton ordered 207,000 portable electric fans from Lasko Metal Products out of Fort Worth, Texas. The order exceeded $2.6 million dollars for the company. Not only was Lasko able to keep the hundreds of workers who were about to be laid off, the Wal-Mart order allowed Lasko to increase its employment by 18 per cent. The fans cost about $13 dollars each. A Korean bidder offered to make the same fan for $10. To let the business community know he was behind the "Buy American" program, Walton opted to go with Lasko. The positive image the deal brought to Walton was the best money he could have ever spent in self-promotion.

In 1983, Wal-Mart imported most of its dress shirts. By 1985, Walton found a company that made a quality shirt at about the same price as the imports. Capital Mercury Shirt Company now supplies shirts not only for Wal-Mart, but also for other retailers as well. The small firm uses very conservative ways to compete with the import companies.

Enterprises like fledgling Murray Corp., a bicycle and lawnmower manufacturer, have also benefited from "Buy American." Walton sold the company's lawnmowers and bicycles exclusively, but the price had to be right. Murray doesn't make as much as it used to from its products, but it is still in business. In the 70s, with a tight economy, people were mowing their own lawns instead of hiring others to do the job, and Americans appreciated the advantages of exercise and fitness. They were buying a record number of bikes. Murray had always made a dependable bike, but the company wanted to compete with Schwinn and other higher priced two-wheelers to gain maximum profits from about the same amount of sales. Faced with Japanese, Korean and Taiwanese products, Murray didn't have the luxury of seeing the kinds of dollars it was hoping for. Wal-Mart and K-Mart helped keep the company afloat by doing business with them and shunning the Taiwanese product.

In many ways the "Buy American" program worked. But when it came to losing money as opposed to selling American-made quality products, Sam Walton went with the imports. When it came to money and profits, Walton was not going to lose a penny. And he shouldn't have to. Any good businessman wouldn't. The "Buy American" program was an ambitious one, but it was not without problems of its own.

Sam began writing a column in the company's newspaper which was aptly named *Wal-Mart World*. In the column, he would tell the employees what he was thinking and what he expected of them. On the "Buy American" program, he had this to say:

"Our Wal-Mart can and should set an example for others in helping the United States out of the very difficult financial situation that we're in. . . . We should initiate an all-out campaign to cooperate with our industries and manufacturers to buy everything possible in the United States. We should assist them to be competitive and more efficient in many ways, and that should be our intent and objective. If done correctly, I am very certain that U.S. workers, if provided the proper equipment, incentives, and participation, can produce merchandise in these United States that will be as good a value, or better, than anything we can buy overseas."

When a major Taiwan distributor of toys and games looked over the "Buy American" program, he knew he had lost his security. If Wal-Mart and others could get a comparable product from an American supplier, he'd be out of a job. Records, tape players and automotive products were all in jeopardy. And with Reagan in the White House, no foreign supplier was safe from American-made goods. American suppliers were working their labor in much the same way as their overseas counterparts, and American prices were coming down while quality was on the way up.

"Taiwan Eddie" (a term retailers use for cheap imported goods), couldn't compete in such a market. Companies like Haggar, a major supplier of slacks to Wal-Mart, May Company and Mervyn's, put together a game plan to fight "Taiwan Eddie." Headquartered in Dallas, Texas, and with plants in Mexico and the Caribbean, Haggar maintained quality while utilizing a cheap labor force. Although Walton had been buying slacks from Haggar for over twenty years, he wasn't happy with the way Haggar did business. But the company managed to keep its costs down through the cheap labor force and still compete with "Taiwan Eddie." Walton would rather see his money go into a company that paid American taxes rather than a company from overseas that didn't.

American business is becoming more and more complicated. Sam Walton knew this and he tried to keep his transactions as simple as possible. When dealing with American suppliers as well as overseas manufacturers, Walton went for the bottom line: price. Even though he was a staunch advocate of "Buy American" he was no champion of the cause. He couldn't afford to be. While Americans were waging a war against overseas suppliers, Walton had to find the cheapest products to fight his competitors in his own trade territory. But the positive publicity Walton received from his small contribution to the "Buy American" cause gave him a wealth of positive exposure for the expansion of the Wal-Mart machine. And as it rolled across America, it became known to all its customers as the all-American place to shop.

15

Sam's Shallow Pockets

Sam Walton didn't get to be the richest man in America by giving his money away. Short of being a miser, Sam would only give money away if the funds were matched by a government entity or if the amount was insignificant. Like his father before him, Sam Walton valued money to the extreme. He remembered the Depression.

After Walton donated the $150,000 to the visitors' center named for his father in Columbia, Missouri, he kept a low profile. With each succeeding year, and after the tax man came, Walton tended to give away more in the name of the Wal-Mart company. The cards and letters were still pouring in for donations from Walton for everything from a person's car wreck repairs to schoolbooks for black youths in Atlanta. But there was no way Walton could fill everyone's needs. After all, it just wasn't feasible.

He was encouraged to "do something" to show he wasn't a greedy old man. In rural America where he was operating, people tend to take things personally. When a billionaire gives $20 to a hundred black kids to shop in his store, it wins the hearts of millions of potential customers. When Walton's name continued to appear in newspapers across the nation as the richest man in the land, that too tended to stick in the customer's mind.

A black kid was caught shoplifting a Sony Walkman from a Wal-Mart store in 1987. When asked why he did it, he said, "Hell, old man Walton won't miss it . . . shit, he's so rich he won't ever know a thing about it."

In an effort to share his wealth with the average American and to show people he was far more charitable than his reputation had implied, Walton and his staff put together a few donations aimed at helping the youth of America and spreading the gospel of free enterprise. Helen Walton, who had always donated heavily to the family church in Bentonville as well as to almost anyone in town who had a legitimate need, was also picking up the pace. Sam and Helen were worth billions of dollars, and spending it became a problem because their personal requirements were small.

Walton's staff leaned towards the educational needs of young people in and around

Arkansas. Under the Wal-Mart umbrella, Sam instigated a $1,000 per store scholarship program for employees who worked part-time at Wal-Mart and wanted to continue their education after high school graduation. When he started the program there were 850 Wal-Marts, and it was an expensive proposition at $850,000 per year. As the store chain grew, Walton spent $1.5 million in 1990 on the program. In reality, it's either give it to the kids or give it to the government in the form of taxes. Walton would rather he gave some of the money to the kids.

In 1986, Walton began a program to aid students from Central America at Harding University in Searcy, Arkansas. He wanted them to learn the ways of democracy and free enterprise. The program would cost him $3.6 million, but there was one stipulation: the government would have to match the donation.

It agreed to do so, and the program has become successful. While visiting in Panama, Walton saw the need to teach the ways of American business to any and all students who come to this country. One student from Belize said he'd like to be the Sam Walton of his homeland. With Walton's help, he is realizing that dream.

On the homefront, Walton's image was weak. Politicians knew he was tight with his money and knew he was a hard sale. In 1984, Sam Walton contributed $7,500 to the Republican party, $4,000 to the Wal-Mart Stores political action committee and $250 to a Democrat who lost a House primary in Arkansas. With that kind of commitment from the nation's richest man, it's no wonder the man lost. Even more astonishing was Walton's meager contribution in the first place.

With pockets so deep he could literally put anyone in office he wanted to, Walton remained a man of little action when it came to political donations. He was overheard at a board meeting stating in effect the politicians of the nation were "lazy and basically calculating" when it came to actually getting any work done. And Sam Walton never paid for laziness.

Walton was long a believer in education. Like most Americans, he was astonished at the school dropout rate of our young people and vowed to fund any worthwhile project dealing with the problem head on. Such a project emerged in 1987 called *Project Second Chance*, a prime-time television documentary shot on location in six states across the United States focusing on the scope of the national high school dropout problem. As part of the Public Broadcasting Service (PBS) literacy emphasis for the fall of each school, the documentary was shown nationally, to help get dropouts into adult education (GED) study programs and earn their high school equivalency diplomas. Walton used money from Wal-Mart to be a part of the program.

"I am pleased Wal-Mart can help support a worthwhile project such as *Second Chance* . . . maybe, in a small way, we can get young people back into the classroom and become productive citizens in America's workplace," he said. The effort was admirable, but again, Walton had the personal funds to do more in the area of hands-on approaches that are struggling to turn the tide in the high drop-out areas of the nation. At least he made an effort. And the mileage he received from airing the program in the cities and towns where Wal-Mart operated was some of the best advertising dollars Walton ever spent. After five years as the country's wealthiest citizen, Walton was doing everything he could—short of standing on a rooftop and throwing money—to shed a better light on his image.

When the Walton home burned down in the early 1970s, Sam was content to spend just enough money to move a double-wide trailer on the land. He proposed to live in the trailer permanently, but, of course, Helen protested. She wanted another home, and Sam relented. He built a small version of the first one and added a few luxuries such as a swimming pool and a tennis court. But true to his nature, Walton was uneasy about it all. Although he was the most conservative billionaire in the United States, the man and his money continued to have a love-hate relationship.

As the nation experienced a drought in 1988, Walton donated 10,000 fans to the elderly to help fight off the heat. Total cost: $60,000. The gesture was praised by President Reagan and made front-page news across the nation. The CEOs of K-Mart and Sears were once again left behind while Walton's company continued to aid its customers on a personal level. Walton didn't have to spend massive amounts of money on advertising. He could spend much less by helping out a few of the less fortunate and get more for his money than the multimillion-dollar ad campaigns Sears and K-Mart were buying to stay one step ahead of him in the retail world.

One of Walton's last charitable efforts before turning over the reins to David Glass in 1988 was a Wal-Mart $1.6 million donation to the Children's Miracle Network. Donations from Wal-Mart and its employees were well-received, and millions of Americans who didn't know what a Wal-Mart store looked like received a positive image of the company. Those people on the east and west coasts were being primed, should Wal-Mart enter their markets for business. In the future, Wal-Mart plans to utilize donations to gain a reputation of community hands-on involvement.

Sam Walton could have built the most elaborate office in America. Instead, his office was small and cluttered. It didn't look like the high-rise offices near Wall Street, nor did it resemble a west Texas oilman's work space. Sam was never one for fancy frills. The simple design of his stores lets the customer know the savings are in the product, not in the fixtures. In 1989, in an effort to fight off the growing Wal-Mart threat, Sears revamped many of its smaller stores to look less expensive. The image Walton projected was one of simple but clean floor space. He always left the carpet to his competitors.

Walton's detractors called him "stingy," while supporters say he was the greatest philanthropist of the past two decades. The truth is a little of both. He had deep pockets when the situation called for it, and he could be as cold as a Sunday night supper if the cause lacked merit. It all depended on the perspective. His image, going into retirement, remained that of virtual sainthood to the more than 100,000 employees who did, indeed, get a paycheck from the richest man in America.

Sam Walton: Private Billionaire

Throughout Sam Walton's business life, he was a millionaire almost from the beginning.

From the day he opened Walton's Five & Dime in Bentonville, Arkansas, in 1950 to the day he attended Wal-Mart's 1,351st grand opening, Sam had an ample amount of money to meet his needs. He and Helen really never had a need that his millions couldn't buy. And the public's perception of his mounting wealth was common knowledge in the areas where he owned a store. But going into the '80s, Walton had become a billionaire many times over. Not many in history have ever reached that goal, especially on their own. What is the difference between a millionaire and a billionaire except a few dollars? In the public's mind, there isn't any difference. Rich is rich. Period.

Privacy was always a necessity for Walton. From the time he was a shy, somewhat intro-verted kid growing up in Missouri to the time he made his first million in the 1960s, Sam always valued his privacy. Unlike many of the world's richest men and women, Walton pre-ferred to stay out of the limelight.

During the 1980s Sam was undecided as to just how he wanted to be known upon his death. In the years ahead, with the many words that will be written about the lives of the very rich, he and others will be heros in the minds of all Americans. With their stories, young men and women will want to work hard and succeed. When they hear of Sam Walton's massive wealth, well into the billions of dollars, they will want to be just like he was. After all, there is nothing wrong with attaining wealth. It's what you do with it after the fact that intrigues the masses.

The
Bright
Horizon

16

Sam's Wholesale Clubs: The Ultimate in Free Enterprise

In 1979, Sam walked into a wholesale grocery store and liked what he saw. The idea of the customer waiting on himself, and products stocked to the ceiling in a no-frills setting, appealed to Walton's sense of overhead. America had known about wholesale stores and clubs for over twenty-five years. Sam decided to put the two together and venture out into the wholesale business. In such an enterprise, the merchant realizes a very low profit margin but makes his money off a high volume of sales. With Sam's Wholesale Clubs, Walton was able to offer the same products he had stocked in his Wal-Mart stores at an even cheaper price.

Everything Sam Walton touched in business

turned to gold. When the first Sam's Wholesale Club opened, small business owners who didn't have wholesale suppliers rushed out to join. The clubs were the hottest thing to hit the urban markets in decades because the small business-man could now buy in bulk and save on shipping and middleman costs. But there was a catch: Walton's fee for joining the club was $25 per member and $10 for each additional card. The cards resembled a driver's license, and Walton was selling memberships faster than he could print the cards.

The clubs were the ultimate in free enter-prise. There are only a handful of businesses in the United States where a customer has to pay up front just for a chance to buy something at a discount. And for the small businessmen and large families who swear by Sam's Whole-sale Club and the money they save, they didn't realize the savings were minimal. Over half the products in Wal-Mart could be found in Sam's, With very little price difference. The only sav-ings members could realize was if they bought in large quantities and bought it all the time. A family can only buy so many tires and televi-sions. In essence, Sam's was a novelty, a status symbol. Walton's marketing of the clubs made them appear the logical approach to modern-day shopping in America.

The clubs themselves require a surprisingly rigid application fee. The member must own a business or be an employee of one. Products are sold on a cash and carry basis, and there are no salespeople out on the floor. It is strictly a "help yourself" deal. A member can buy boxes of toilet paper or a thousand hamburger patties. He can buy jeans or car batteries. Many small businessmen buy goods from Sam's and resell them at their stores. The warehouse pricing cuts out the freight and the wholesale supplier usually associated with small business buying. Most of the merchandise is still in boxes, ready to pick up.

A strange quirk, one that Walton devised to make Sam's appear exclusive and encourage membership, is that no one is allowed in the store without a membership card. There is a greeter at the door who checks to make sure the shopper has a card for entrance. When the person leaves, the sales slip is checked to verify the items were purchased by a valid member. This exclusive treatment made Sam's desirable and the talk of the more than forty cities in which the clubs operate.

Sales at Sam's Wholesale Clubs were staggering right from the beginning. In the past, there had been value clubs much like Sam's, but his down-home ways made shoppers feel they were dealing directly with a person, an older man, the neighborhood grocer of their childhood. Sales increased 62 per cent over three years to $2.11 billion. Sam's opened 35 units in 1988, and the growth of this brainchild is endless.

To expand the club into new areas, Sam bought out 17 Super Saver Warehouse Clubs, which were dying a slow death. These 17 units accelerated Sam's position into the club market and by 1988, he was the number one whole-sale club merchandiser in the nation. He even started a newspaper entitled *Sam's Buy-Line* to advise members of the company's growth and sales prices. The small publication paid for itself by selling advertising to product sup-pliers. How's that for making money at every turn?

Warehouse clubs began in the late 1950s as deep-discount distributors. It was just a mat-ter of time before huge retailers like Walton would enter the market. They combine the effi-ciency of a warehouse with the volume of a dis-count store. Sol Price, the former owner of Fed-Mart, a chain no longer in business, opened his first club in San Diego in 1976. In 1990, Price Co. earned $46 million on sales of $1.9 billion. Sales for the entire club industry were $4.4 billion a year, which so far accounts for one per cent of all United States retail sales. In 1989, those figures doubled.

What distinguished Sam's Wholesale Clubs from Wal-Marts was the way Walton handled the inventory. At Sam's Walton tried to unload the merchandise before he had to pay for it, usually in thirty days. Typically, a successful warehouse turns over its entire inventory on a monthly basis, about four thousand items, with little or no net investment. By contrast, an average discount store has to keep $3.5 million tied up to stock $7 million dollars worth of inventory. Walton could earn sixty per cent on his investment with a Sam's outlet as opposed to twenty percent in a Wal-Mart outlet.

Sam's Wholesale Clubs tend to be located in more obscure places where the rent is low. About twenty-five per cent of their sales are grocery items; twenty per cent, appliances; and the remainder is a hodgepodge that includes office supplies, apparel, tires, hardware, and even satellite dishes. Prices that average just eight to ten per cent over cost, about one-third the typical cost at Wal-Mart, keep the entire stock moving out the door. The actual profits come from holding down operating costs. Sam's buildings are usually larger than two football fields, double the size of the largest Wal-Mart. Little or no advertising, very few employees, and the occasional delivery make Sam's a very profitable business. Members usually come up to the store in trucks or vans to load up.

One drawback Sam saw in the few years he was in the business was that competition is getting tougher by the day. Small, independent companies and big-league corporate players were challenging Price and Walton.

Four independents went public to finance a massive expansion. Costco Inc. of Seattle, Pace Membership Warehouse of Denver, Warehouse Club Inc. of Skokie, Illinois (twenty per cent owned by W.R. Grace) and Wholesale Club Inc. of Indianapolis pledged to build fifty additional warehouses this year to compete with the rise in Sam's Wholesale Clubs. Sam planned to stay in the market—he liked that sixty per cent—and expected to open thirty or more stores a year. Kroger became the first supermarket company to join the action when it bought the five-store Price Savers chain in August 1987. Zayre Corp., a Massachusetts discounter, initiated a massive expansion of its BJ's Wholesale Club division, a company still trying to turn a profit. BJ had only eight clubs on the east coast and was no direct threat to Sam's territory.

With so much competition, an industry shakeout appears inevitable. To break even, a wholesale club needs to have a volume of sales amounting to about $35 million per store per year. Only two companies to date have more than $50 million a year in sales per store: Price and Sam's Wholesale Clubs.

Although the club industry's trailblazing years aren't over yet, the window for entry is slamming shut. Security analysts point out that the off-price retailing business as well as wholesale clubs are beginning to reach their peak. But Sam's future looks bright, because they only sell the latest merchandise. Joseph Ellis of the investment banking firm of Goldman Sachs summed it up this way:

"Wholesale clubs like Price and Sam's are the single most important new distribution concept to come along since Wal-Mart and K-Mart began discounting in the early 1960s." Discounting produced some remarkable success stories in those days, along with some spectacular blowouts. It's a scenario that is likely to be repeated as the wholesale club race heats up in the 1990s.

Sam's Wholesale Club is different than its competitors, mainly because the millions of customers who shop at the more than 1,400 Wal-Marts across the nation also are members of Sam's. They are loyal to Sam's and feel they knew him. Working class citizens living in the breadbasket of America as well as the Bible Belt don't like spending their hard–earned money on strangers who stay in ivory towers back east. They either spend it with the average Joe, or they'd rather not spend it at all.

Walton gave them two avenues to buy from him, Wal-Mart and Sam's. When the tale of the tape is added, it's easy to see Sam Walton was the average Joe to consumers living near a Walton outlet. And they are spending their money with Sam at a record rate. There literally is no end in sight.

17

Wal-Mart's Expansion

Under Rob Walton and David Glass, with new blood in the company, Wal-Mart will become the number one retail outlet in the free world. As Wal-Mart's first $6 million dollar associate, Glass has some incredible ideas for the future. A highly educated and motivated man like his predecessor, Glass has already, in two short years, opened Wal-Mart up to areas where Walton only dreamed of doing business. Using the same conservative approach, Glass will expand Wal-Mart only if the company pays its own way. Once a store fails to do this in any marketplace, the expansion will stop. The east and west coasts of America are still no-man's-land for Wal-Mart. So was any city with a population of over 200,000, until 1990.

Sam Walton dabbled in other retail endeavors over the years after the first Wal-Mart opened in 1962. In 1983, he opened the first dot Discount Drugstores in Des Moines, Iowa (purposely using the small letter "d" to show its bottom-line price promise). In 1985, a second dot was introduced in Kansas City, Missouri, and in 1986, he opened two more locations in Shawnee and Wichita, Kansas. There are now twelve dot Discount Drugstores operating in four states. Once again, Walton proved that taking discount prices to rural and medium-sized cities would start a tidal wave of profits and launch a new, successful enterprise.

The three Helen's Arts and Crafts were becoming, however, a burden to operate even though they were profitable. Sam decided in 1987 to sell the three stores to Michael's Stores, Inc. of Irving, Texas, in an effort to ease his workload. There is no doubt with enough time, the Walton family could have made the arts and crafts chain into one of the nation's largest.

By 1987, Sam owned 1,400 Wal-Mart Discount Stores, 105 Sam's Wholesale Clubs, 12 dot Discount Drugstores and 3 Helen's Arts and Crafts. Not only was he the richest man in America, he was the biggest retailer in the nation in terms of companies owned. His massive portfolio was the most impressive of its kind . . . he was virtually a company within a company.

One of the most ambitious ventures of which Sam Walton ever became a part occurred in

1988 when he opened the first Wal-Mart Hypermart in Dallas. Hypermart, from the French work "hypermarche," describes a megastore which sells food and nearly every kind of general merchandise and service available. It's the largest and most popular newcomer to the retail in America.

"If these stores are successful, they could change the face of retailing in America just as they have in Europe," said Norm McMillan, a retail planning consultant who heads his own firm in Chicago. "But we do not think their success is a lead-pipe cinch, even though it has been instigated by the legendary Sam Walton,"

"Hypermarket is nothing more than a code for 'my own private shopping mall,'" offers Sid Doolittle, a partner with McMillan. "And it's easy to see why Walton would want to get into a business like this with the potential of $100 million a week in sales for one store."

The hypermarket setup is massive. With 220,000 square feet of retail space, it's the size of a major-league baseball field and a football field combined. There are groceries on one end and a garden center next to an automotive center on the other. In between, there is a huge toy store, men's and women's and children's clothing, a drug store and a deli. At the entrance, there are fast-food outlets. Although Sam Walton never intended to get into the food business, to make the hypermarket idea work he needed to include it to offer the complete store.

Regional grocery chains such as H.E.B. Food Stores and Walton worked together by putting H.E.B.'s successful enterprises next to Walton's equally successful dry goods operations. This enables the shopper to make one stop for both food and clothing. Wal-Mart also worked with Dallas-based Cullum Co, a giant food retailer, to aid in the success of hypermarkets in Topeka, Kansas, and Kansas City, Missouri.

Sam also developed and opened several Wal-Mart Super Centers in conjunction with food retailers in various states to get the maximum dollar out of the buying public while offering the one-stop approach as an easy way to shop.

Wal-Mart's expansion is a positive mandate of the commitment Walton made for the future of his retail empire well after he is gone. His children and his grandchildren may never need to work a day in their lives by virtue of the powerful and massive retail world he built for them from the ground up.

18

Wal-Mart/ Wall Street

One of the most fascinating aspects to Sam Walton's achievements was how he stood in the eyes of Wall Street. Just how did Walton and his empire stack up in the eyes of those in the know? Well, Wal-Mart is the darling of Wall Street. While the biggest companies in the world overtake each other with regularity, Wal-Mart is the constant many brokers tend to suggest to anyone wanting a solid investment.

Each and every year since it arrived on Wall Street, Wal-Mart has enhances its high profile. Stock bought in the early days of the company rose over 100 per cent in the shortest time on record. In May 1988, Wal-Mart reported net retail sales for the previous month of $1.58 billion. With some $20 billion a year in sales, Wal-Mart continues to out perform its competitors on Wall Street.

Wal-Mart (WMT), like most major U. S. companies, couldn't stop the events of October 20, 1987. The Dow dropped 508 points as stunned investors saw the worst crash since 1929. Wal-Mart stock, forever strong, took a beating along with such blue chip stocks as IBM and Exxon. Many Wal-Mart employees were sad to see their personal total fall like a rock in the sky. Even citizens who had no direct link with stocks as a whole could be affected through their jobs. It was a horror story for all.

Never in the history of the stock market has one man lost so much in one day as Sam Walton. Being the richest man in the nation and owing 39 per cent of Wal-Mart stock, Walton lost $2.6 billion dollars in net worth on October 20, 1987. With a total personal fortune at around $8 billion, Walton's remarkable wealth was able to withstand the drop. What's two billion when you've got eight? More amazing, Walton didn't appear to be overly rattled by it all. Time and time again he told the press, "It's only paper." This time, Walton lost one hell of a lot of paper.

Wal-Mart's Stock Purchase Plan (the "Stock Plan") was adopted in 1972 to make available to eligible associates (employees) of the company and its subsidiaries a means of purchasing shares of Wal-Mart common stock on the New York Stock Exchange at market prices not to exceed $1,500 per year. Wal-Mart contributes an amount equal to 15 per cent of each participation employee's contribution under the stock plan.

Many of Wal-Mart's associates are well-versed in Wall Street lingo and keep their eyes on the stock. Many believe the stock will be their "nest egg." With turnover at the management level almost nil, floor employees, knowing they would never get the top job at their respective locations, looked upon their Wal-Mart stock as their salvation.

Wal-Mart's profit-sharing plan is one of the best in the industry, and many hourly employees participate after the mandatory one-year probation period has passed. Arthur Young and Company of Tulsa, Oklahoma, Wal-Mart's independent public accountants and auditors since Wal-Mart began offering securities to the public in 1970, gives a yearly accounting of Wal-Mart stock at the company's shareholders' meeting.

At one such meeting, Sam Walton told the crowd that he'd do a hula dance on Wall Street if the company had a pre-tax profit of 8 per cent in 1983. When the final tally was in at 8.04 percent, Walton donned a grass skirt and leis, and danced the evening away to the sounds of Don Ho. It was a sight to see, and it was the first time Walton let his hair down in public.

The future for Wal-Mart as it grows will no doubt make it one of the most sought-after stocks on Wall Street. Just as Exxon, IBM and General Motors are considered solid investments based upon their decades of doing business in the black, so will Wal-Mart. It will be the number one retail stock for many years to come.

Sam Moore Walton: Personal Awards

1978

Received Top Retailing Awards. Man of the Year and Discounter of the Year. 1978: Became the second retailer inducted into the Discounting Hall of Fame.

1977–78

Forbes magazine ranked Wal-Mart as number one in the retail business in the following categories: Return on Equity. Return on Capital. Earnings Growth. Sales Growth and Profitability.

1982

Wal-Mart was recognized as one of the Five Best Managed Companies in the nation by

Dun's Business Review. (In 1987, Wal-Mart was again recognized by Dun's as one of 15 honorable mentions as Best Managed Company).

1984–85

Wal-Mart cited in management books *In Search Of Excellence* and *A Passion For Excellence* by Tom Peters. 1984: Sam Walton is named the recipient of the Horatio Alger Award. He is also at the top of *Forbes* 100 Richest Americans list.

1986

Awarded the Golden "Chief Executive Officer of the Year" by *Financial World* magazine for the Best in All Industries. 1984, 1986: Awarded the Silver Award by *Financial World* magazine for the best in Consumer Goods and Products.

1981, 1982, 1984, 1986, 1987

Awarded the Bronze Award by *Financial World* magazine for Best in Retail.

1987

Again, Sam heads *Forbes'* list of 100 Richest Americans with a personal worth of some $8.7

billion. Awarded the Libertas Award for free enterprise achievements by Enterprise Square, USA, American Citizenship Center, Oklahoma Christian College.

1987

Inducted into Oklahoma Hall of Fame for free enterprise achievements.

1988

Winner of the Gold Award by the National Retail Merchants Association, the first time a non-member had taken the honor.

1988

Recognized by *Business Month* as one of the Five Best Managed companies for the years of 1972–1987.

1989

Winner of the CEO of the Decade Award from *Financial World* magazine, New York. Acknowledged by *Discount Store News* as the Retailer of the Decade, December 1989. Editors of *Mass Market Retailers* named Walton and his "associates" as Mass Market Retailers of the Year. 1990: Named as one of the top ten Most Admired Companies in America by *Fortune* magazine (tied for sixth overall with PepsiCo).

1992

Winner of the Presidential Medal of Freedom. President Bush and his wife, Barbara, flew out to Arkansas to publicly award Sam Walton.

Epilogue

Before I began this project, I wanted to know what the public thought of the richest man in America. I hired a firm to do a survey and received some interesting answers. First, many didn't know who Sam Walton was, but they knew the richest man in America was the man who owned the Wal-Mart store chain. Many thought President Ronald Reagan was the richest man in America, and a few thought either Donald Trump or Lee Iacocca had to be the richest man alive. It was an interesting lesson on just how little information the media had printed about Sam Walton. The media had failed to place him in the public eye long enough for the public to know anything significant about him.

Not only did I have the privilege of working for Sam Walton at a time when he was putting the company together, but I had also met him on a few occasions informally. In 1986, when I began my search for the Sam Walton I had met in the past, I contacted him about the possibility of helping me with a biography of his life. He wrote to me less than two weeks later:

Dear Mr. Teutsch:

Last week I received your letter about the possibility of a book on my life. First, I want to thank you for the personal compliments included in that letter. I am flattered that you think enough of me to want to write a book about my life, and I appreciate very much the positive picture of me which you seek to present to your readers.

As you know from being a past Wal-Mart employee, I have always attempted to protect and preserve my privacy as much as possible for myself and my family. In fact, several people have suggested that I write my own story. I guess if "my story" is going to be told, I would prefer that "someone" to be me. For the reasons of my privacy, I am asking you to reconsider your biography of my life. Although I wish you every success in your writing career, I would be most appreciative if you chose another subject at this time . . .

In closing, I again want to thank you for your interest in myself and Wal-Mart and I hope you understand my position of not wanting a book published at this time.

Thanks for giving me your attention and consideration. My best wishes as you continue your writing career.

Very truly yours,
Sam M. Walton

I hesitated, then bowed to his request to postpone the writing. It wasn't until 1988, after hearing of his handing over the reins of the company to David Glass that I decided to go on with the project. I knew that sooner or later, someone would put together something on his life and I wanted to be a part of it, having worked for Wal-Mart Stores. No one can know Sam Walton's ways without having worked under his system.

It was clear to me the reasons why Sam didn't want me to continue writing this book, but I felt the time was right. America, in my opinion, needed all the success stories it could get. By 1988, after Sam had moved away from the company, he was becoming restless, and the idea of writing about his life began to appeal to him more and more. He contacted me about the progress of my work. When he learned I had all but finished the manuscript, he found a writer from a major business magazine to aid him in writing his own account. It seemed Sam was finally set to come out of his shell. On a sad note I knew that he had been battling bone cancer for a couple of years. With the help of this business writer, and after a four-million dollar advance from a well-known New York publisher, Sam Walton was ready to tell his story. His final letter to me read:

Dear Mr. Teutsch:

I'm happy to hear your business is doing well and that my philosophy as far as retailing is concerned has been of some help to you. I'm also flattered you still have an interest in getting your biography of my life into print.

A little news of my own: I have finally decided to put my views in writing and am currently under contract with Doubleday to do so. A writer has agreed to assist me with the project which is presently underway. I wish you well in your writing and thanks for staying in touch.

Best wishes,
Sam Walton

Between this book and his own account of his life, due out sometime in 1992, America should get a clear picture from two different perspectives of the life of the richest man in America.

Sam Walton died April 5th, 1992, at the age of 74. The bone cancer he had fought so gallantly for five years had finally taken its toll. But his massive legacy lives on. Even though the Walton fortune was split among family members at Mr. Sam's request in 1989, it remains the largest family fortune in America today, amounting to some $22 billion in net worth. The family also retains 38% of the Wal-Mart/Sam's Wholesale Club fortune.

Sam Walton never made himself an easy man to reach. Should you be curious to take a look at his beginnings, which are the subject of a museum in the Wal-Mart headquarters town of Bentonville, Arkansas, you'll have a long trip: first by plane to Little Rock, the state capital, then by small plane to Fayetteville, and then by car some twenty miles into Bentonville.

Before Mr. Walton's death in April of 1992, President George Bush and his wife, Barbara, took that long journey to publicly give Mr. Sam the Presidential Medal of Freedom before a teary-eyed crowd at the company headquarters. Mr. Sam, in a wheelchair and wearing a Wal-Mart baseball cap, accepted the award, the nation's highest civilian honor, with a broad smile and an extended hand. He even demanded to stand up, with the help of Helen, his wife of 50 years, to greet all those present, just as if he were conducting one last pep rally.

Some people wonder if President Bush, who had never visited Arkansas before, and who at this writing seems most likely to run for re-election against Arkansas Governor Bill Clinton, made the trip for political reasons. I believe this was not the case. Mr. Walton was too ill to make the flight to the White House and it was an honor Mr. Bush had wanted to give for some time. Some three weeks after the Medal of Freedom was bestowed, Sam Walton was dead.

What becomes of Wal-Mart, the largest retailer in the free world? Who will continue Mr. Walton's dream of good service and low prices for the next generation? Who will keep the heat on the competition? Just what is going to happen now that Mr. Sam is gone?

Not to worry. Mr. Sam raised his oldest son in his own image. Two days after the death of his father, Rob Walton stepped into Sam's shoes to run the largest retail company in America. David Glass, Wal-Mart's President and Chief Operating Officer, will continue in that capacity. There was no great power struggle here. Wal-Mart stock didn't take a nose dive at the news of Sam Walton's death. In fact, it's business as usual with Rob at the helm. A lawyer, forty-seven year-old Rob Walton has long played a strong role in the company's real estate development and site selection for Wal-Mart's expansion. The recent move to the larger cities, head to head with Sears and K-Mart, as well as plans to move into the Northeast, were in large part due to work done by Rob with the help of David Glass.

A 1969 graduate of the Columbia University School of Law, Rob Walton served as Wal-Mart's general counsel and secretary from 1969 to 1982. He joined the company's board of directors in 1978 and became Wal-Mart's senior vice-president. There is little doubt that Sam Walton planned this event as he planned everything relating to Wal-Mart and its position in the retail world. In the hands of Rob Walton, a man more than capable of handling the job, Wal-Mart will continue to grow and succeed. Sam Walton left nothing to chance. ◄

So what did I learn from Sam Walton's way of doing business? And what can you, the reader, do to make your life better in the ever changing business climate we all seek to succeed in?

I looked at the basics of Wal-Mart: 1. Good service with a smile 2. Find a need and fill it. I did both with my business in Austin, Texas. Our first year, with two stores, we grossed $300,000.00. As we added stores, our sales went to the million-dollar mark. Mine is not a retail business. But I saw a need and I filled it: I sold convenience and I did it with a much-needed product and a smile. Time and price are the key ingredients to success in today's marketplace. Even though you will work twelve-to-fourteen-hour days, as I have and Mr. Sam did, the payoff is tremendous. Hard work and dedication are the key to present-day competition. No one is going to hand you anything. No one is going to give away their "inner secrets to their success"— unless they are trying to sell you seminars or tapes. Believe me, believe Sam Walton: making it in business takes hard work, dedication and a service or product that the public demands. All the elements have to fall into place for a business to become a Wal-Mart or an IBM or a General Motors.

There is something to be said for hard work and fourteen-hour days. The most successful men and women go that extra mile to achieve more than the average worker. They want more and they're not satisfied with less. Sam Walton was never content with being number two on the list. From his childhood Eagle Scout medal to his first Wal-Mart Discount City in Rogers, Arkansas, in 1962, thirty years ago, Walton wouldn't take a backseat to anyone. In the years to come, there is little doubt that Wal-Mart will expand in some capacity to many countries of the world.

Sam Walton will go down in the annals of retail history as one of the greatest success stories in American business. Never in the history of our country has there been a man who so lived the American dream from the time he was born. Sam Walton defined that dream. He had his faults as everyone has, but he didn't let them get in his way. He was a man on a mission and he succeeded like no one before him. I just hope the next great businessmen and women will achieve their dreams with the same class and style that Sam Walton kept as he achieved his. His example gives the rest of us something to hope for in our own lives.

About the Author

As a former employee of Sam Walton, with a background in journalism from the University of Arkansas, Austin Teutsch found himself in the unique position to compile and write Mr. Walton's life story. Having worked for Mr. Walton at the ground level during the time the massive Wal-Mart empire was being built, Mr. Teutsch knows the "Wal-Mart Way" first hand.

With many published articles in magazines and newspapers throughout the United States, Mr. Teutsch set out to find the richest man in the land. In *The Sam Walton Story*, Teutsch spent two years in seven states getting to the heart of the man who took the American dream to biblical proportions.

Mr. Teutsch currently resides in Austin, Texas, with his wife, Martha, and their young son, Taylor.